T0013363

KAMA
SUTRA

A POSITION
A DAY

KAMA SUTRA

A POSITION
A DAY

Illustrated by
Alicia Rihko

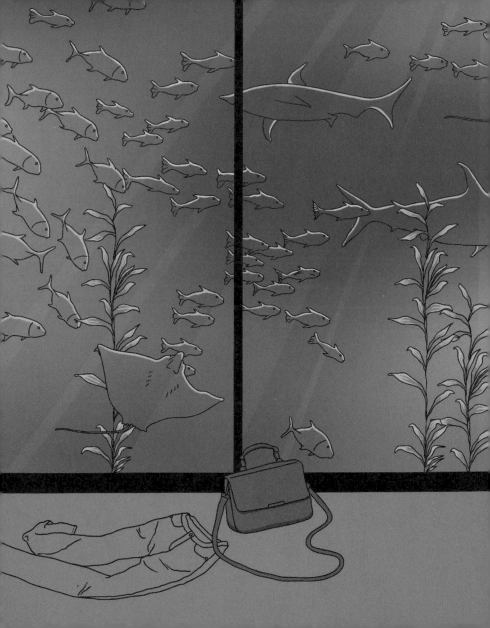

CONTENTS

INTRODUCTION

Since time immemorial, we've loved
spicing up our sex lives with a little
variety. Have you ever wanted to dazzle
a new lover with your wicked invention?
Or refresh the long-cherished intimacy
you hold with the familiar love of your
life? Or try something totally new just
for the fun of it? As it turns out, so did
our ancestors.

Here, you'll find a position for every
day of the year, inspired not only by the
most famous love text in history, but by
other classic authors. Who hasn't heard
of the Kama Sutra? Written sometime
between the 2nd and 5th centuries by
the great yogi Mallanaga Vatsyayana,
its aim was not just to share naughty
secrets, but also to reflect on the whole
nature of pleasure, love, and how to live
a fulfilling life. A grand work indeed, but
not the only word on the subject: here,
you'll find tips from other classics—the

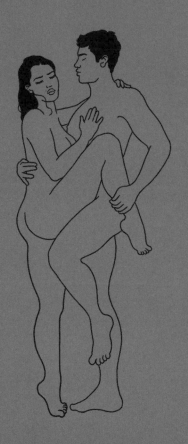

Smaradipika, the Ananga Ranga, the Panchasayaka, and the Ratikallonlini—books written by poets, scholars, and philosophers to enlighten lovers across the ages. If all that sounds scholarly, don't worry: you and your partner are all you need to bring to the table ... or bed, floor, staircase, or anywhere else you fancy.

People are sexy creatures, whenever or wherever they're born, and we love to experiment. We all know that different positions are one way to shake things up. Sex is a physical conversation, and the stance you strike at the beginning can do a lot for your tone. But there's more to it than just different twists and angles. Human beings are creative, and we like to work together making new and beautiful things. As the ancient writers taught us, sex can be part of that: to try new ideas in bed is to sculpt with sensation, to paint with love. Artists of former times knew that sex could be an art.

There are lots of ways you can read this book. You can leaf through, looking for a new favorite and trying whatever catches your eye. You can take on the huge and hilarious challenge of attempting one position every day—and whether you succeed or not, there's no question you and your partner will be happier, funnier, and closer for giving it a shot. If you're after something specific, you can also flip to the end, where you'll find a Random Selector pointing you toward our particular recommendations for whatever mood you're in.

Some of these positions are sensual, sleepy, or spiritual caresses. Some of them are limb-bending, brow-raising feats to make you feel tingly and bright all over. All of them are a door to a creative playground where you and your lover can run wild.

THE
POSITIONS

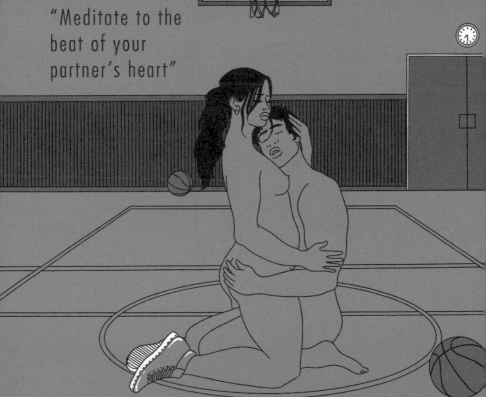

DAY
001

THE PULSING EMBRACE

A loving and sensual
full-body caress.

"Meditate to the
beat of your
partner's heart"

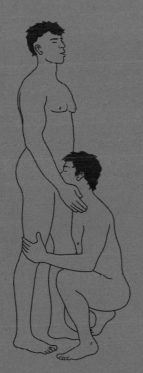

DAY 002 | THE ALMOST-KISS

The Kama Sutra says this is for young virgins, but don't let that stop you.

"A fluttering breath of temptation"

DAY 003 | SUCKING THE MANGO STONE

A timeless way to their heart.

"The delicious full-mouthed swallow"

DAY 004

ROLLING THE PEARL

Lightly massage with fingertips on either side, moving in gentle counterpoint.

"Treasure your partner's clitoris with delicate skill"

DAY
005

THE SNAKE EMBRACE
Eyes closed and heads averted,
experience pure sensation.

"Twine together
in unthinking
bliss"

DAY
006

THE KNIGHT'S SALUTE
No need to kiss chastely—
let your lips and tongue
plead your case.

"A courtly gesture
no one can resist"

DAY 007

KSHOBAKA (STIRRING)

The Kama Sutra describes this lapping movement as drinking at their sacred fountain.

"Stir your tongue between their wide-held thighs"

DAY 008

THE CUPPED BOWL

Fingertips at the base of
the skull are chaste but
astonishingly intimate.

"Succumb to
a state of
pure nurture"

DAY
009
LOVERS' GREETING

A wonderful way to reunite, no matter how long you've been parted.

"So happy together, you could dance on air"

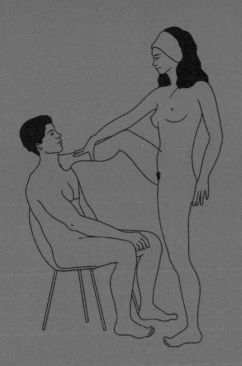

FLAUNTING THE PRIZE

This is one for the true show-off.

"See, yearn ...
wait for their word"

THE BRAIDED REEDS

A sleepy, sensuous caress for lovers newly acquainted.

"Twine thigh to genital
and twist in mutual delight"

DAY
012

LOVE'S FLAG

Let yourself grow light-headed
with sensation as they thrust.

"Raise a salute
to your passion"

THE PESTLE

A delicious chance for them to
let their hips do the talking.

"Lie still while your lover
grinds you to ecstasy"

THE LIFTING VESSEL

A vibrant position
for the one on top
to free themselves
from shyness.

"As one drinks at
their lover's delta,
the other drinks
pure air"

DAY
015

PIERCING THE DARKNESS

Don't be shy: tell them how
much you love this.

"A flare of
excitement that's
sure to dazzle"

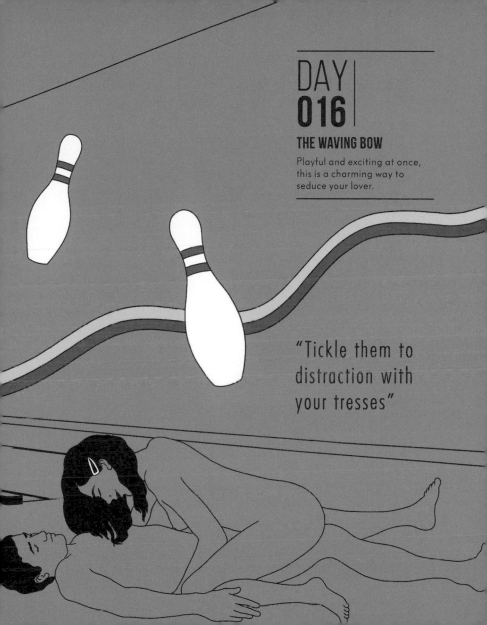

DAY | 016

THE WAVING BOW

Playful and exciting at once, this is a charming way to seduce your lover.

"Tickle them to distraction with your tresses"

DAY 017

FOREHEAD EMBRACE

For a meditative thrill, focus only on those places where you touch.

"Caress mind to mind in a gentle embrace"

DAY 018 | MILK AND WATER
An embrace that can melt without warning into lovemaking.

"Press together so your bodies seem almost to penetrate one another"

DAY 019 | THE STRAY CUR'S TRICK
A naughty nip goads them into punishing you.

"For extra fun, get on your hands and knees, staring at them provocatively"

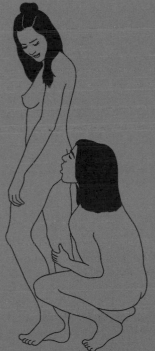

DAY
020

THE WILD BOAR

A little caution: as the Kama Sutra says, save this for moments of intense passion.

"A fierce bite
to mark your
beloved's skin"

THE CIRCLING TONGUE

The Kama Sutra advises you to probe with your nose and chin, as well as your mouth.

"Wind and wind around until their head spins"

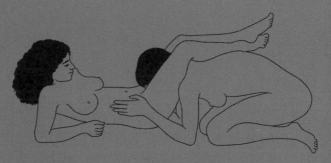

THE STORM CLOUD

Gentle but firm, a tease to bring passion to a lightning frenzy.

"A light circle of marks on a beautiful breast"

DAY 023

THE SEAT OF SPORT

A sweet position recommended by the Smaradipika.

"Play together with innocent delight"

DAY
024

THE PARTED WAVES

A comfortable position
for easy entry.

DAY 025

WINDING THE THREAD

With each downward stroke, add a little twist over their most sensitive point.

"A turn of the hand to entangle their heart"

DAY 026 | THE FOLDED LILY

Comfortable but vigorous, a favorite for loving couples.

"Pleasure your partner until they bloom with ecstasy"

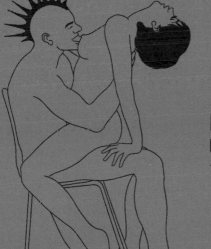

DAY 027 | DRINKING THE DEWDROP

A light lick and suck that makes even the shyest lover eager.

"Make your beloved thirsty for more"

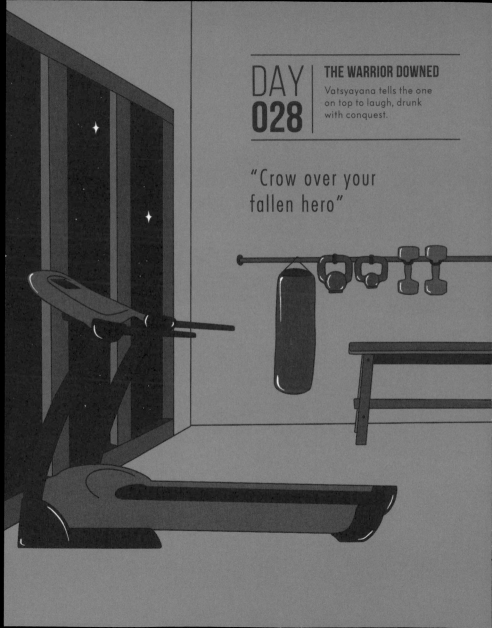

DAY 028

THE WARRIOR DOWNED

Vatsyayana tells the one on top to laugh, drunk with conquest.

"Crow over your fallen hero"

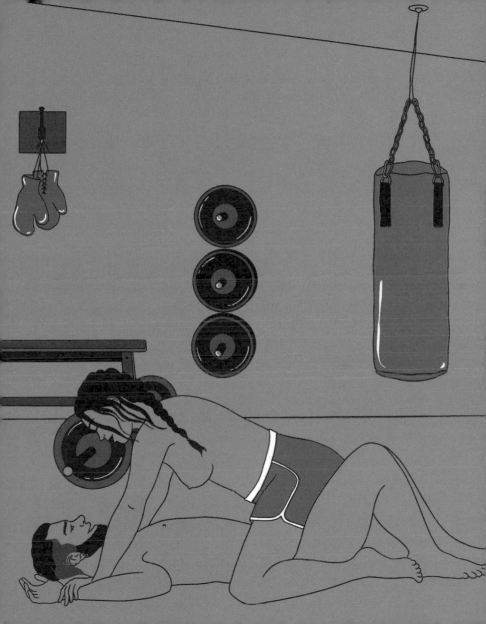

DAY
029

| **THE MARE'S TRICK**
The Kama Sutra says this takes lots of practice; Dr. Kegel would add that's a fine idea.

"Squeeze and stroke them inside your vise"

DAY
030

| **THE ATTENDANT**
Enjoy your partner's tender touch and lovely legs in perfect ease.

"Form a circle of caressing head to feet"

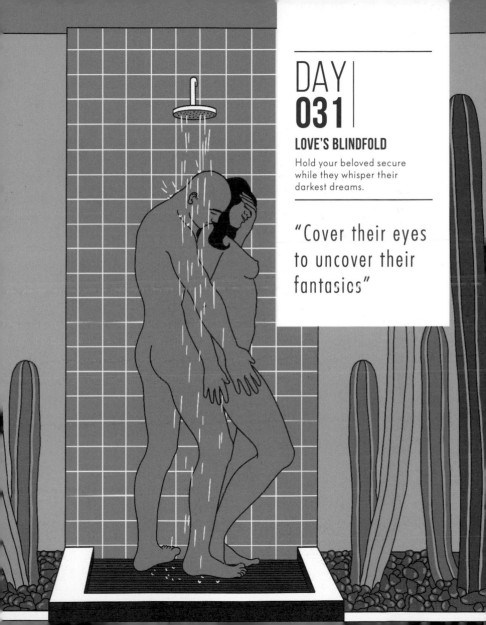

DAY 031

LOVE'S BLINDFOLD

Hold your beloved secure while they whisper their darkest dreams.

"Cover their eyes
to uncover their
fantasies"

DAY
032

CHUSHITA (SUCKED)

The Kama Sutra suggests you add some nibbling as well.

"Draw deep kisses from their well of pleasure"

DAY 033

THE OPEN-HANDED STRIKE

A light slap to the sternum that startles the body into passion.

"Tread the breathless border between pain and pleasure"

DAY
034

THE LINE OF DOTS

Bite gently, but enough to leave
a mark they can cherish.

"Decorate them
with a secret
memento"

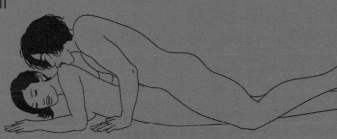

DAY
035

THE PEACH HOLD

Rest against your lover,
thinking of nothing but
their circling hands.

"A delectable massage
for succulent
breasts"

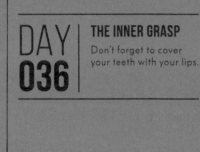

DAY 036

THE INNER GRASP

Don't forget to cover
your teeth with your lips.

"Hold them hard for a moment before releasing"

THE ROWING BOAT

A position that's at once fun and tender.

"Rock, rock, rock with your beloved"

THE WILD HORSES

With one foot loose, clasp your lover's hips for steadiness so you can move freely.

"A vigorous position that shakes your body into a frenzy"

DAY
039

CASTING THE GRAIN

With your legs bent
back, you can thrust
with unexpected force.

"Buck underneath
your partner to
scatter their wits"

DAY
040

THE PEACOCK'S TAIL

For those who can manage it, this gives a stretched, wide-open sensation.

DAY
041

AFTER THE JOURNEY

Don't forget that life is a
voyage together, so do
this often.

"They'll travel
far for a treat
like this"

DAY
042

THE SQUEEZE

A swift yet tender caress for new lovers building their intimacy.

"Press together suddenly, shocking the breath from each other"

DAY
043

THE TIGER'S CLAW

The Kama Sutra suggests nail-play is particularly thrilling before and after a long separation.

"Rake your mark across your prey's flank"

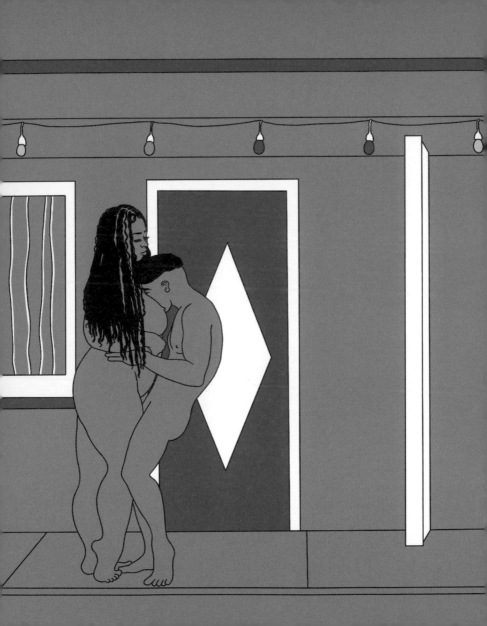

DAY | 044

THE FLOWER GARDEN

A soft, silky, sensual treat in which many find utter bliss.

"Bury your face in sweet-scented softness"

LEOPARDESS KISS

To make a game of
it, nip them lightly
if they squirm.

"Knead and
groom your
prey"

TWINING OF THE CREEPER

An embrace that suits both gentle
and passionate moods.

"Twist and nestle
together, free-standing
like dancers"

DAY 047

EMBRACE OF THE JAGHANA

A hold that presses each jaghana (middle part of the body) against the other.

"Caress belly to belly, melting into each other"

DAY 048

PRASRITAKA LOVE-BLOW

Cupping the hand cushions the impact, so this is great for playful swatting.

"Curl your hand into a snake-hood shape and strike"

DAY
049
THE VICTORY

A good grip on each other's legs gives a feeling of security to this position.

"Ride together, glorying in your passion"

RIDING THE TONGUE

Let the rider lead the way
while you honor them with
your tongue.

"Squirm and dance
over your lover's
moving mouth"

THE LOVER'S
HEARTBEAT

A sensual meditation
for true romantics.

"Tap to the rhythm of
your partner's pulse
and feel the boundaries
between you melt"

DAY
052

THE FOOT YOKE

Holding your partner in
place can be thrilling at
the height of passion.

"Catch your
ankles and trap
them close"

PLUCKING THE PETALS

One that can be tried with or without lubricant for different sensations.

"Tug gently at their lips to release their nectar"

THE LONG CARESS

Holding the leg in place, the caressing one strokes gently as far as their fingers will go.

"Thigh to chest, relish your lover's fine flesh"

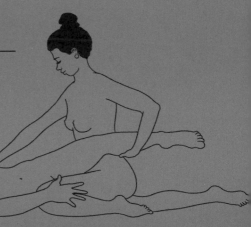

DAY
055
THE APPROACH

A caress that can easily slip into deeper pleasuring as the lovers' hands wander.

"Slide into a sensuous embrace"

DAY 056

THE KISSING GAME

If you lose, Vatsyayana says to protest that your lover cheated and you want another chance.

"Vie to capture each other's lower lip in mischievous competition"

DAY 057

THE FEEDING BIRD

A ticklish delight for the sensuous.

"Pluck little kisses from their palms and soles"

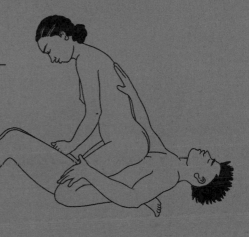

DAY 058 | THE MILKMAID'S PATIENCE

Pause a little at the end of each stroke so your partner is always on the brink of climax.

"Draw long strokes of pleasure until they beg for release"

DAY 059 | THE DOUBLE HOOK

A chair can serve to steady you when you're too excited to find the bed.

"Catch each other in a moment of impulse"

DAY 060

THE BAMBOO GROVE

Excellent for deep penetration or, if you prefer, for anal.

"Enter between sweet, soft limbs"

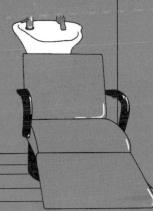

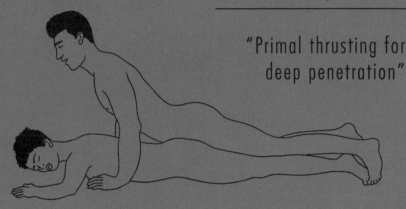

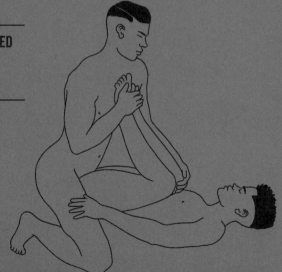

DAY
061

UNION OF THE ELEPHANT
A position that tests the strength of the one on top.

"Primal thrusting for deep penetration"

DAY
062

THE HIGH PRESSED POSITION
A wild position for energetic lovers.

"Cast away all restraint and let desire overwhelm you"

DAY 063

BAHUCHUSHITA (SUCKED HARD)

They can quickly escape if the sucking gets too much, so go at it with enthusiasm.

"With all the force of your lips, work your lover to please them"

DAY
064

THE RUDDER

A chance for the penetrating
partner to show off their
strength and flexibility.

"Holding tight
to your partner's
legs, steer yourself
to climax"

DAY | 065

CAPTURING THE MAIDEN

Those of good aim may find
themselves inside their partner
before they reach the bed.

"Sweep them off
their feet and
into fantasy"

DAY 066 | THE WIDE YAWN

The Kama Sutra advises entering your lover gently in this position.

"Open yourselves to headlong excitement"

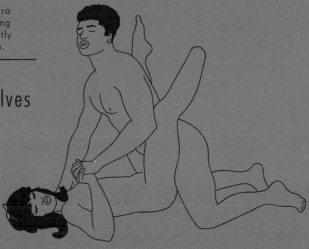

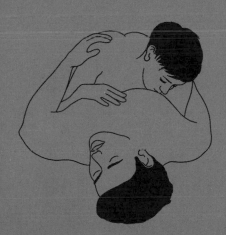

DAY 067 | THE KISS THAT AWAKENS

Mount lightly so they first feel you as your lips touch their skin.

"Coax your beloved from the depths of sleep to the heights of passion"

DAY 068

SPLITTING THE BAMBOO

The penetrating partner kneels astride one of their lover's legs and embraces the other.

"Entwine yourselves and race to pleasure"

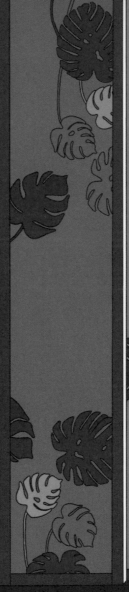

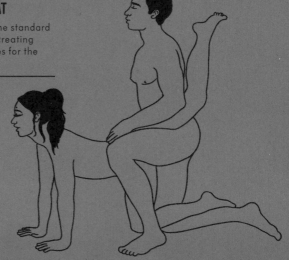

DAY 069 | CLOSING WINGS
A kind courtesy after a position that wearies them.

"Rub your partner's tired shoulders until they drift off to sleep"

DAY 070 | THE TWISTING CAT
A lithe variant on the standard all-fours, good for creating interesting pressures for the one penetrating.

"Flick up a limb for extra enjoyment"

SAMATALA LOVE-BLOW

The Kama Sutra reminds us that love-blows are a matter of taste, so be sure your partner is willing before you try.

"Give your lover an open-palmed slap to feed their passion"

DAY 072

SCALING THE PASS

Penetration may be tricky, but with some massage oil, you can rub blissfully against their stomach.

"Ascend your lover's body to truly delight in their shape"

DAY 073

THE REVERSED SWALLOW

Carefully guarding the teeth with the bottom lip will protect the receiver from harm.

"Admire your lover's beautiful form as they pleasure you deep"

DAY 074 | THE FURROW
The Kama Sutra calls it unchivalrous to go on a journey without leaving at least a few scratched mementos.

*"Streak little tracks
in their waiting skin"*

DAY 075 | THE CHEST EMBRACE
A thrilling way to enjoy each other all over.

*"Slide together,
hands forgotten"*

DAY 076

THE SCULPTING CARESS

Pressing your body against
theirs while you stroke
unites flesh and spirit
in tenderness.

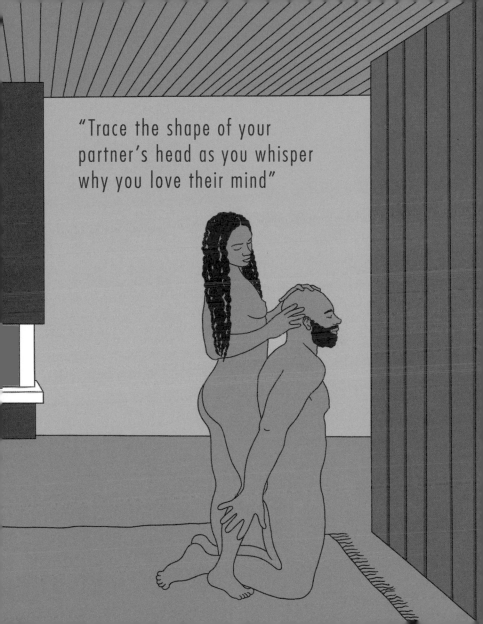

"With all exposed, let your
tongue wander freely"

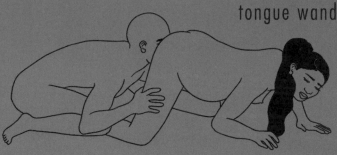

DAY | **OPENING LOVE'S PAGES**
078 | An affectionate pose that
allows your lover to relax and
be explored.

"Study their secrets with
your learned fingers"

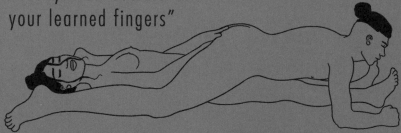

DAY | 079

THE CLING

A tiring position to sustain, so take full advantage and go all out while it lasts.

"Hold hard and tight and thrust full-speed"

DAY | 080

THE QUEEN ASCENDANT

An uncommon pose for the one penetrating: they should surrender and enjoy the novelty.

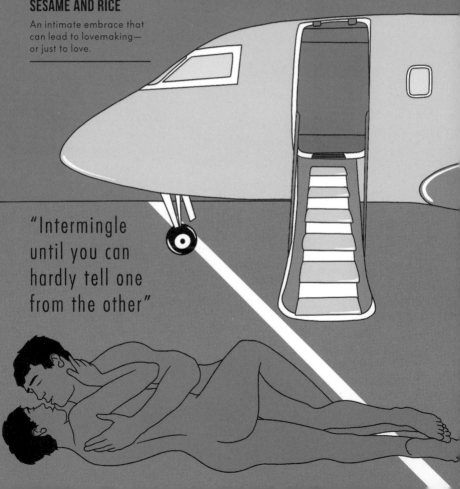

DAY
081

SESAME AND RICE

An intimate embrace that
can lead to lovemaking—
or just to love.

"Intermingle
until you can
hardly tell one
from the other"

DAY 082 | THE SECOND CUP
A convenient position to lick around their delicate anus.

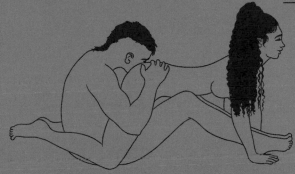

"Ply their secret places with your tender tongue"

DAY 083 | THE RAISED FLAME
A well-placed pillow can be the very thing to achieve the perfect angle.

"Build up your fire with a little support from below"

DAY
084
NIBBLING THE LYCHEES

Pluck lightly at their balls until
your beloved is all in a twist
with anticipation.

"Sweet-seeking lips
are always a thrill"

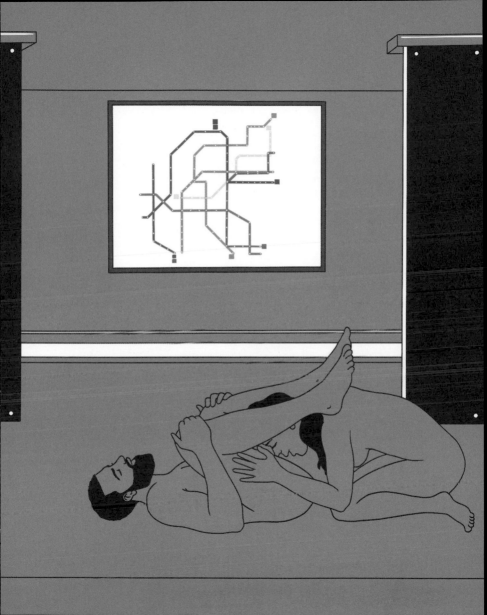

DAY 085 | THE SIGHTLESS MAIDEN

Closing your eyes, explore your lover's muscles and bones through pure touch.

"Feel the warmth and shape of each other in blind bliss"

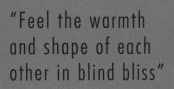

DAY 086 | THE CONCH

A braced and bracing stance that allows for deep penetration.

"Thrust to the rhythm of the ocean until both your bodies echo with joy"

DAY | 087

FEIGNING INDIFFERENCE

A particularly good game
for after-argument sex.

"One thrusts, the
other looks away
and pretends to
ignore their
partner"

DAY 088

THE WINE PRESS

Thrusting can take it out of you, but a clever lover knows how to keep their partner refreshed.

"Lean deep to crush the tension out of your partner"

DAY
089

THE ANTICIPATED KISS

Stroke first what you will
kiss later, and your lover's
attention is caught.

"Your fingers press
the hope of sweeter
pleasures into their lip"

DAY
090

PLAYING THE SITAR

Tender and romantic but also sexy and exciting: a true lovers' favorite.

"Hold your graceful partner and let your fingers pluck"

DAY
091

SWALLOWING THE STALK

A skill that most need to practice, but those who master it are unforgettable.

"Open up your throat and take your lover in"

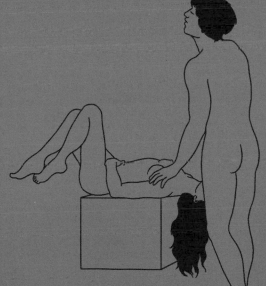

DAY
092

HALF-PRESSED

A position of mutual
power: one thrusts deep,
while the other controls
the distance between you.

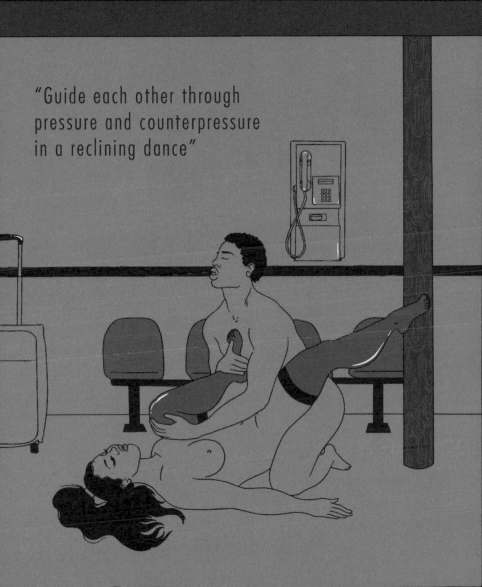

"Guide each other through pressure and counterpressure in a reclining dance"

DAY **093** | **THE VALLEY OF DESIRE**
Between the balls and anus is an oft-neglected treasure—pay it good attention and listen to the gasps.

"Ply your tongue on their most secret sensitive spot"

DAY **094** | **THE FLYING FISH**
All the thrusting falls to the one penetrating; let them enjoy the control.

"A tingly, floaty break from gravity"

DAY 095

OPENING THE HEAVENLY GATE

For those who love their toes nibbled, this is a revelation.

"Deep penetration and silken kisses play in divine counterpoint"

DAY | 096

THE ORCHID

A position in which to rock gently, taking care of each other's comfort.

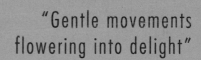

"Gentle movements flowering into delight"

DAY 097

THE SPOKED WHEEL

The challenge of the pose raises self-awareness as the one being touched enjoys their pleasuring.

"Balance together in elegant harmony"

DAY 098 | DIPPING IN THE INKWELL

If they don't like having their navel tickled, you can just threaten to do it and watch them squirm.

"A cultured lover knows when to tease"

DAY 099 | THE RAFT

A pleasantly stable and easy variant on the feet-off-the-ground position for the one being penetrated.

"Drift into delight on your lover's lap"

DAY 100

THE BAKER'S PLEASURE

Someone who attends to their lover's shoulders will always be welcome in their bed.

"Knead their delicious flesh until they rise to your touch"

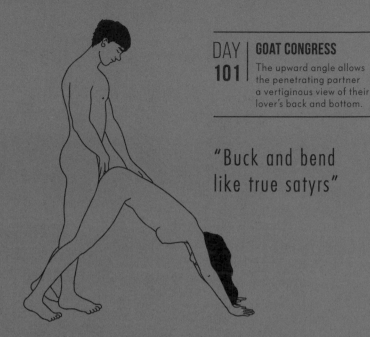

GOAT CONGRESS

The upward angle allows the penetrating partner a vertiginous view of their lover's back and bottom.

"Buck and bend like true satyrs"

THE JUMPING CRICKET

A position for playful lovers looking to challenge their bodies.

"Leap together until you chirrup in delight"

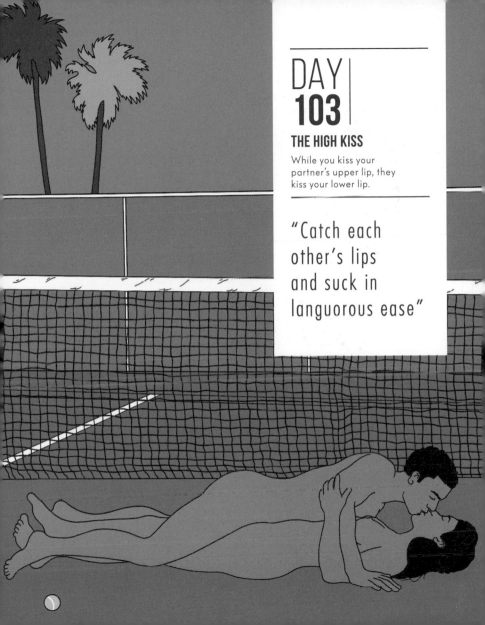

DAY | 103

THE HIGH KISS

While you kiss your partner's upper lip, they kiss your lower lip.

"Catch each other's lips and suck in languorous ease"

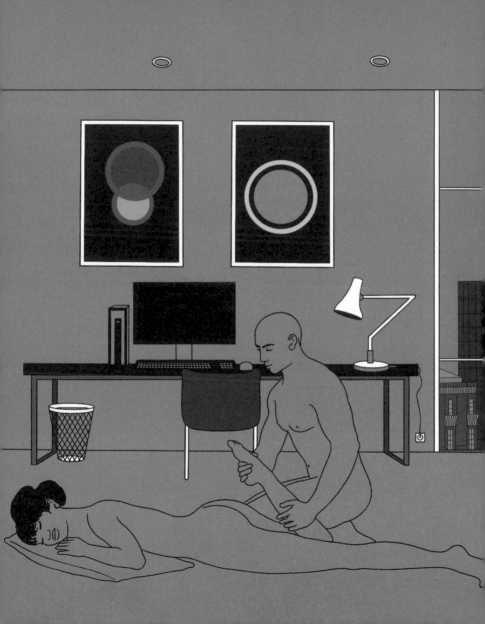

DAY | 104 |

BENDING THE REED

True relaxation for the one being massaged that will always make them appreciate their lover.

"Turn your partner's sweet calf upward and massage at your leisure"

DAY 105

THE CROW

According to the Kama Sutra, the Crow is so much fun that many a courtesan abandoned patrons who wouldn't indulge in it.

"Take your lingering, licking, luscious time"

FORCING THE GAZE

If they turn their eyes aside, gently steer their face and coax them to look at you.

"Break through shyness to love"

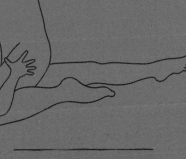

HALF JEWEL CASE

A springy position that allows for deep enjoyment.

"One treasuring their lover's whole body has wealth indeed"

DAY 108

THE GLANCING CONGRESS

An embrace best tried
on a soft floor for a good,
stable base.

"Angle your bodies apart
to luxuriate in the cool
air on your skin"

DAY 109 | THE POTTER'S WHEEL

As your partner revolves on your hips, you can caress their beautiful thighs.

"Spin yourselves to a pinnacle of excitement"

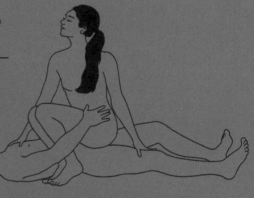

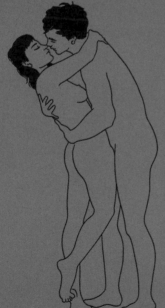

DAY 110 | THE BENDING EMBRACE

If your hold is strong, this can be a deeply passionate embrace.

"Press down on your beloved and shower kisses"

DAY 111

LOVE FLICKERING INTO FLAMES

A delicious experience that can kindle any kind of lovemaking.

"Gazing at your beloved's face, you kiss them to wakefulness"

DAY 112

RISING POSITION

A clever lover knows how to tease their partner's clitoris with their thumb from this stance.

"Thrusting upward, the couple floats toward climax"

DAY
113

THE CIRCLING CARESS

At once arousing and
soothing, this is a fine stroke
for deepening love.

"Let them drift
into a dream of
sensuality"

THE GRASS BLADE

A marvelous way to startle them into uninhibited laughter.

"Tickle them from below with your soft-stemmed tongue"

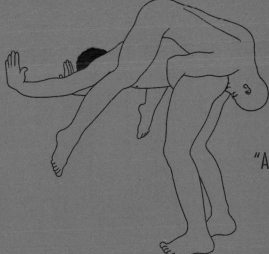

THE TORTOISE SHELL

A challenge for the one standing to keep steady as their excitement builds.

"A beloved partner is no burden if their hands wander to delicious places"

DAY 116

TILTING CONGRESS

Good support for elbows and knees adds greatly to the penetrated partner's comfort here.

"It's easy to be overwhelmed when you're off-kilter"

THE COBRA LEAVES THE NEST

A tricky and roguish position for lovers who like to laugh together.

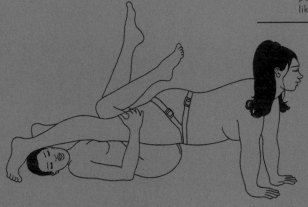

"Slither up and out — and in again"

THE TOWN WAY

The Ananga Ranga teaches that this is a favorite for the artistic.

"A simple treat for the sophisticated lover"

DAY | 119

THE RICKSHAW

A position that tests the muscles, to be tried in a comfortable setting.

"Those with strength and vitality can draw their lover down paths of endless pleasure"

DAY
120

THE TAUT RECIPIENT

The strain of this pose can help drive the one receiving toward an intense orgasm.

"Get their muscles and their passion all worked up"

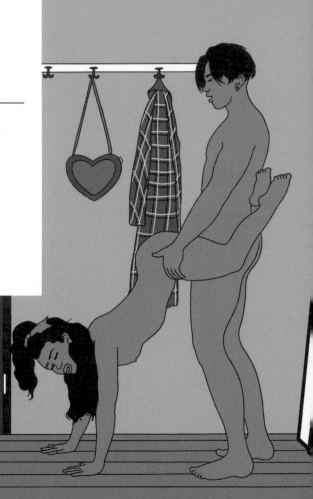

DAY
121

BEAUTY INVERTED

A position for the
penetrating partner to
show all of their vigor.

"Display
shameless
admiration of
your tipped-up
darling"

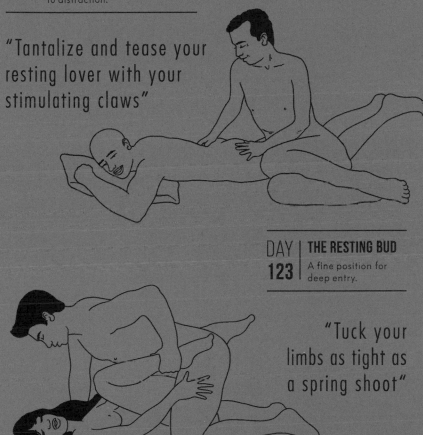

DAY 122 | THE KNEADING KITTEN
Alternate massage and light scratching to drive them to distraction.

"Tantalize and tease your resting lover with your stimulating claws"

DAY 123 | THE RESTING BUD
A fine position for deep entry.

"Tuck your limbs as tight as a spring shoot"

DAY 124

AZALEA KISS

A chance to explore the delicate skin of the anus, as well as the clitoris and yoni.

"With your lover's treasures right before you, you can quest with tongue and lips"

DAY
125 | **THE SWIFT'S NEST**
An energetic but
affectionate position for
pleasure to take flight.

"Fly safely home
into your beloved"

DAY
126 | **CRADLED EMBRACE**
A tender and
wonderful caress for
the resting couple.

"Passion distills
into pure love"

DAY 127

BREAKING THE COLUMN

Come up behind your partner and kiss the back of their knee until their legs give way.

"Even the most elegant form bends to this temptation"

DAY
128

THE LIFTED PLOW

This requires strength in the one being penetrated but allows their partner to thrust fast and hard.

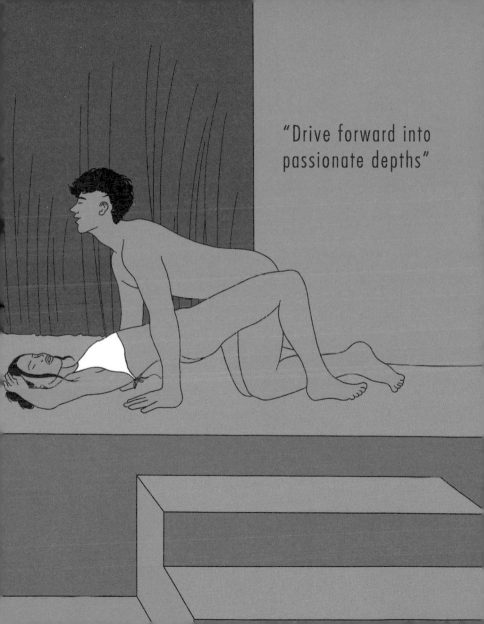

"Drive forward into passionate depths"

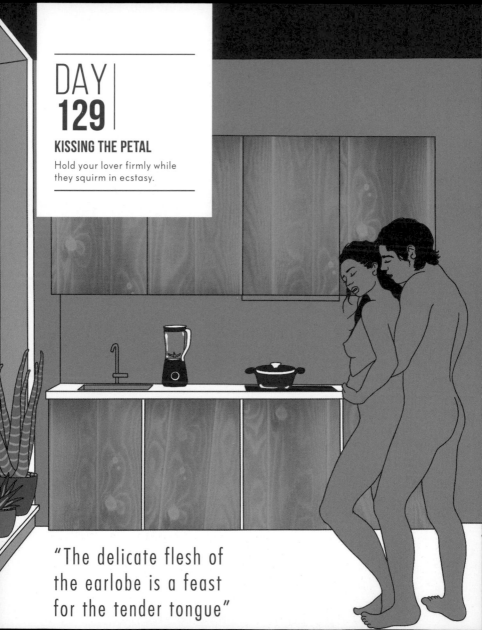

DAY
129
KISSING THE PETAL

Hold your lover firmly while
they squirm in ecstasy.

"The delicate flesh of
the earlobe is a feast
for the tender tongue"

DAY
130 | **THE PATTERING KISS**
A romantic sequence that can
go anywhere on a lover's body.

"Rain one salute
after another on
their satin skin"

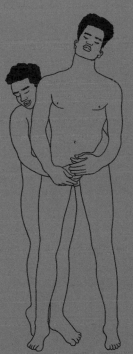

DAY
131 | **TWO HANDS AT WORK**
Use lubricant for smooth,
unbroken flow.

"Slide up one, then
the other for
constant arousal"

DAY
132

SLIDING STRIKE

A vigorous yet careful stroke, particularly good for when your lover is feeling open.

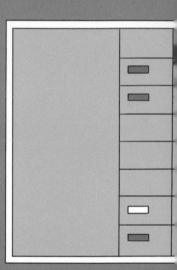

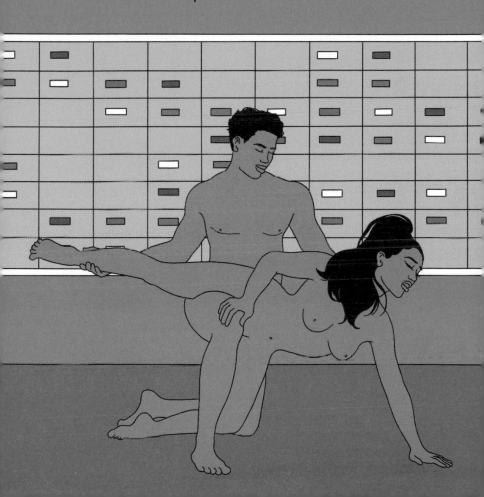

"Slip in slow and pull out fast
in a sweet reverse rhythm"

DAY 133 | THE TRIPOD

The Panchasayaka defines the Tripod as the penetrating partner holding one of their lover's knees while caressing them.

"A rough and ready stance for lingering strokes"

DAY 134 | THE MIRRORED FLAME

A position suited to embraces, where you can admire your partner in all their glory.

"Match each other limb to limb to ignite your tenderness"

THE TUMBLED HOLD

An unusual angle that lets
lovers explore new thrills.

"Hold your
lover entirely as
you penetrate
them deep"

DAY 136

THE TREMBLING KISS

A light, exploratory kiss—
save your tongue for later.

"Nibble lightly
until anticipation
shivers into
pleasure"

DAY
137

CHUMBITAKA (KISSING)

Hold the sucking and lavish
all your attention on their
sensitive underside.

"Round your
lips and kiss
passionately"

THE LIONESS

The Kama Sutra says you can choose which animal you pretend to be, so pick a great one.

"Thrust deep and let loose your primal roar"

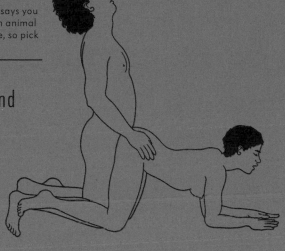

THE TUMBLERS

If you get comfortable, this allows for deep penetration, but fooling around can be fun, too.

"A feat of balance to show off to each other"

DAY 140

THE TRAPPED DOGS

A playful embrace to explore each other genital to genital.

"Press yourselves together in animal curiosity"

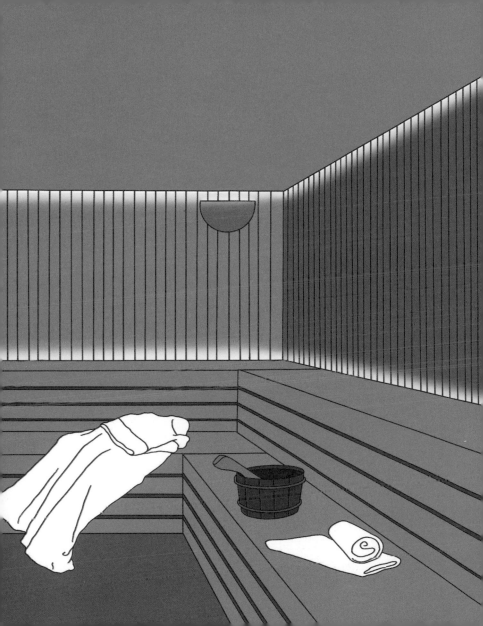

DAY
141

THE HALF CLASP

A comfortable
position for slow,
loving congress.

"Wrap each other in
languid sensuality"

DAY
142

THE FOAL'S KISS

A fun way to get your
beauty's attention of
a morning.

"Nestle up
behind them for
a good nuzzle"

DAY
143

THE NEW LEAF

A way to fill your romance
with the joys of spring.

"Furled around
their lover, the
one on top
grows tender"

DAY | 144

THE TURNAROUND

Particularly good if your erection naturally angles downward.

"A grinding, glorious twist"

DAY 145

THE NESTING CROW

A comfortable variation
on an old favorite.

"Let your lover
mount to the
heights"

THE RECLINING WRAP

This embrace lets you appreciate your lover's lush legs while nestling your genitals close to theirs.

"Hold your partner's thighs and enjoy their flesh"

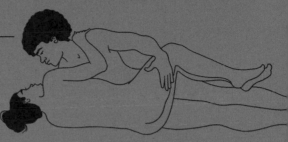

THE STEADIED MAN

In this posture, the penetrated partner acts as an anchor, while their lover controls the movement.

"Lean against a wall as your lover grinds their hips to pleasure you both"

DAY
148

THE TABLE OF PLEASURE

The penetrating partner should have a stool to brace themselves, as this position is taxing.

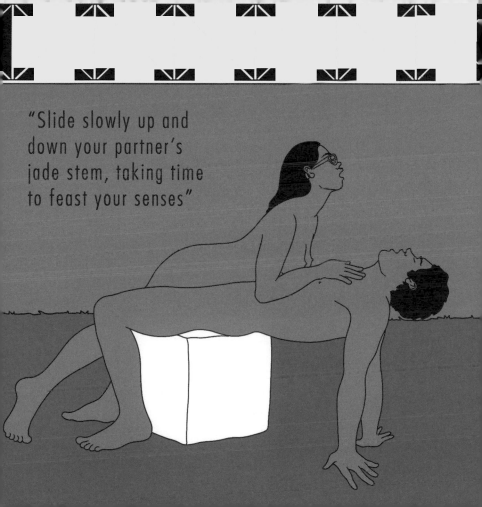

"Slide slowly up and down your partner's jade stem, taking time to feast your senses"

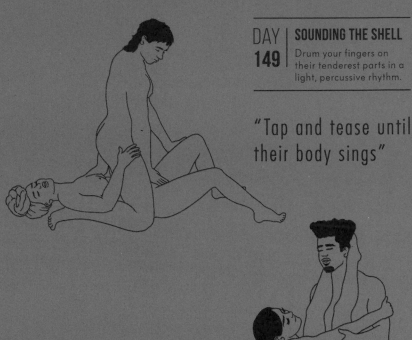

"Tap and tease until their body sings"

"Take a good grip and challenge gravity"

DAY 151

THE SUNDIAL

The tension of keeping your leg straight tightens your muscles to sculpted perfection.

"No shadow can fall on pleasure this bright"

DAY 152

LIFTING THE GODDESS

If you can keep a good
grip with your legs, your
partner's hands are free
to pleasure you.

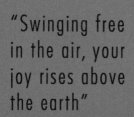

"Swinging free
in the air, your
joy rises above
the earth"

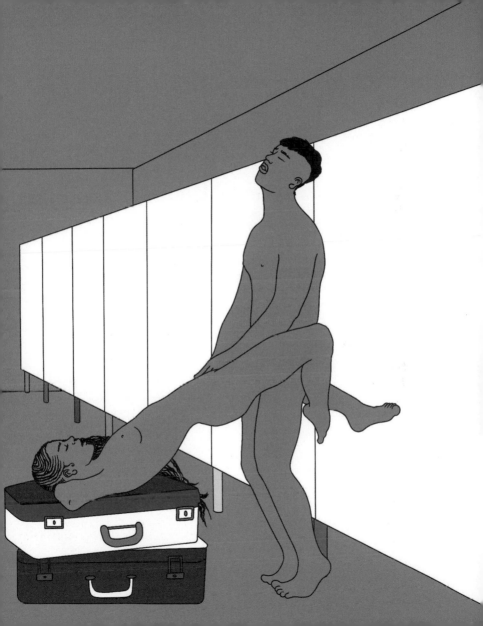

DAY
153

THE HARROW

You might slip out if you try this too fast, so move at a good, measured pace.

"Dig deep and slow in their soft furrows"

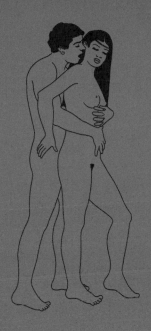

DAY 154 | **KISS OF BREATH**
Don't quite kiss: just let your breath tickle your lover's stretched skin.

"A shivering, sensuous thrill"

DAY 155 | **HALF-CURLED**
A position that suits anal penetration as well.

"Wrapped lightly in your lover's legs, press forward"

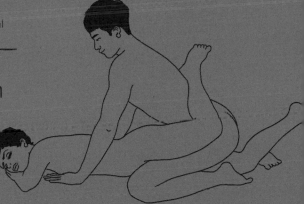

DAY 156

THE DANCER'S APPROACH

The curve of your spine raises your breasts proudly against them.

"Stretch into your lover's lap with regal grace"

DAY
157

THE ARABESQUE

The one penetrating should take a steady stance and be sure to hold their lover securely.

"A dream of pleasure and a dream of grace combined"

DAY
158

THE EAGLE'S PERCH

A pose that tantalizes your partner's desires while impressing them with your strength.

"Breathless anticipation before the downward swoop"

DAY 159

LOVE'S STOOL

If you're limber enough to sustain this, the rush of blood to the head is thrilling.

"Offer yourself up for absolute exposure"

DAY
160

THE NECKLACE OF CORAL

The Kama Sutra suggests pressing only with the upper incisors.

"Wind branching loops of love bites around your lover's neck and shoulders"

DAY 161

THE SAILOR'S PROW

From this position, the one beneath can admire their lover's back and bottom while enjoying the touch of their breasts.

"Feel the motion as you ride secure against your lover's thighs"

THE SLEEPING KISS

In a few minutes, they wake up primed and passionate.

"Stir their dreams with your lips"

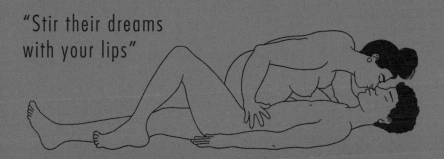

LOVE'S KEYS

The crossed keys of their feet hold your head, so you must gaze at them.

"The cunning artisan unlocks their lover's desires"

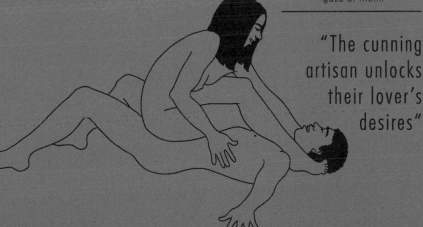

DAY 164

THE BARROW

This is one of the most natural and easy variants on the lifted-partner theme.

"Guide your beauty to a free-wheeling climax"

DAY 165 | THE RUSTIC

It can be easy for the one penetrating to slip out of their partner in this one, but rubbing against their clitoris is just as lovely.

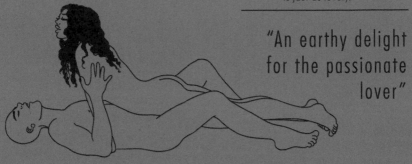

"An earthy delight for the passionate lover"

DAY 166 | THE PULLED KNOT

Experienced lovers use the Pulled Knot for variation in lovemaking, moving in and out of the position.

"Strain against each other to heighten the intensity of your connection"

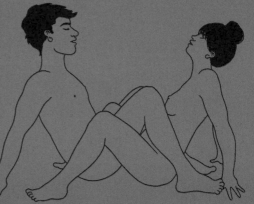

DAY | 167

THE FLYING CROW

Of course, there are easier ways to do this, but it's good to try a real challenge sometimes.

"Chance it and see if your excitement takes wing!"

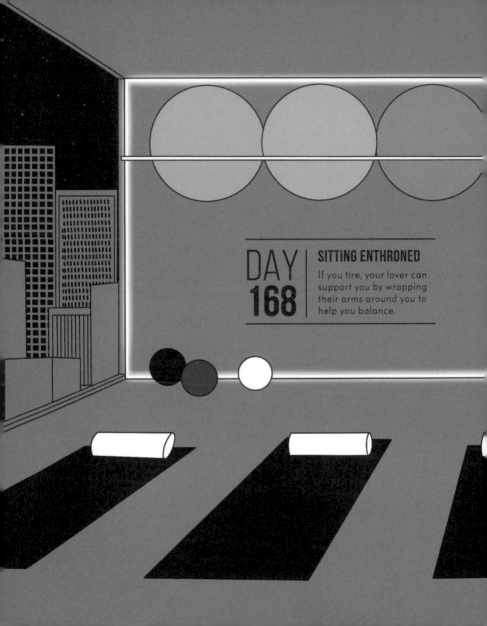

DAY 168

SITTING ENTHRONED

If you tire, your lover can support you by wrapping their arms around you to help you balance.

"Resting impaled, the partner on top squeezes their muscles around their lover"

THE FALLEN LEAVES

A sweet and tender position for loving partners.

"Rest one atop the other and rustle together slowly"

DAY 170 | PALM STRIKE

Pull back your fingers so just the hard flesh of your palm makes its impression.

"Build up a rhythm, making love to their skin"

DAY 171 | THE CREEPING CAT

A comfortable stance that allows for affectionate role-play.

"Arch and rub against your master"

DAY 172

CHURNING CURDS

For an easier alternative, try resting on a good, sturdy table.

"Sink in with slow, fierce delight"

DAY **173**

THE SPLIT SWING

Challenging to the muscles but peaceful in mood, this is one for lovers who know each other well.

"Rock back and forth against each other, keeping blissful time"

DAY **174**

THE SAFE CRAFT

The penetrating partner can brace their feet against something solid to help them hold their lover securely in position.

"Rock together on an ocean of pleasure"

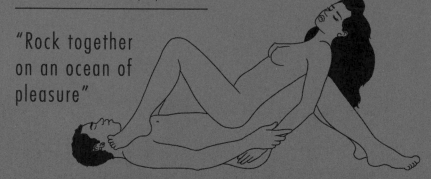

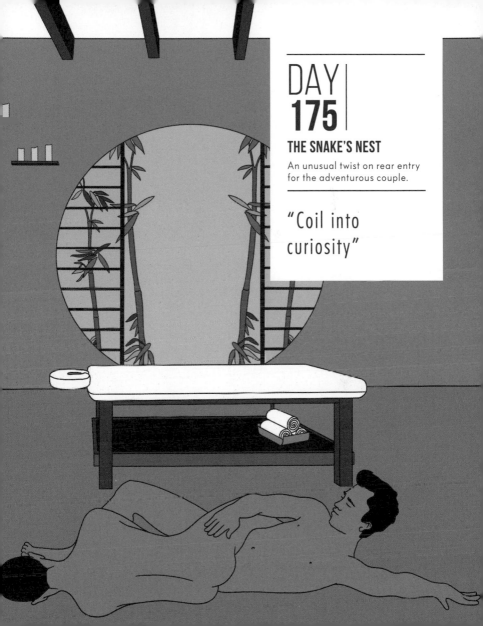

DAY
175

THE SNAKE'S NEST

An unusual twist on rear entry
for the adventurous couple.

"Coil into
curiosity"

DAY
176
REVERSED PROP

A lover's writhing back is a
warming sight, so aim for
a good view.

"Bolster yourself
for a beautiful
vista"

DAY 177

THE DOUBLE BOW

When the one on top holds
their chest still and grinds
with just their hips, this is
particularly exciting.

"Pull your bodies taut
and feel them strum
against each other"

DAY 178 | THE HORSEWOMAN'S EMBRACE

Penetration can be a little uncertain like this, but there are few more enchanting caresses.

"Throw your leg high around your lover and pull them to you"

DAY 179 | SANDING THE GEMS

The nipples can be a fast path to passion, so pay them their due in full.

"Grind their nipples diamond-hard"

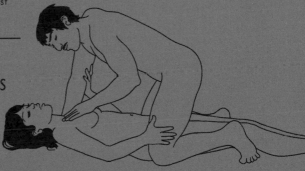

DAY
180
STEERING BLIND

You may love to gaze, but try closing your eyes and meditating only on what you feel.

"Hold fast and become pure sensation"

DAY 181 | TUGGING THE SILK

Make sure you get a good handful, as trapping stray hairs can hurt too sharply.

"A playful pull can excite your lover"

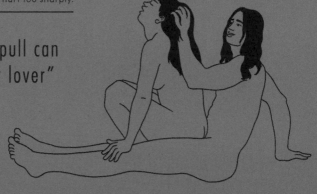

DAY 182 | SKY-FOOT

Recommended by the Ananga Ranga and the Panchasayaka, this is one for deep thrusting.

"Become a firmament unto yourselves as you grow lost in passion"

DAY
183

THE RISING LAMB

A position for you to enjoy the
sensation of your own beauty.

"Pointing one toe,
the one on top
brings elegance
and spirit to
the moment"

DAY 184

BRUSHING THE STALLION

Those who maintain their lover's hard-working muscles will reap a handsome benefit.

"Be a good groom and tend to your mount"

DAY
185

THE DUCK'S WINGS

Folding back the arms
like this displays the breasts
to wonderful advantage.

"Plume
yourself on
your beautiful
bust"

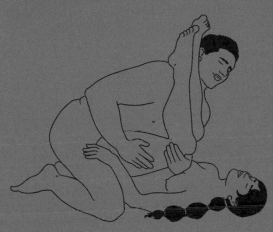

DAY | **THE NUTSHELL**
186 | A position to remember if you and your lover have only a single bed.

"Bend your limbs and crush as close and cozy as you can"

DAY | **THE BEE**
187 | The Kama Sutra advises that this needs practice, but it can be honey-sweet if done well.

"Circle your hips until both of you are buzzing with pleasure"

DAY 188

LOVERS' DELIGHT

The Smaradipika suggests that the penetrating partner lets their hands wander and caress.

"Your heart beats against your lover's heels"

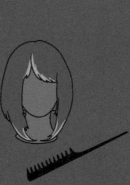

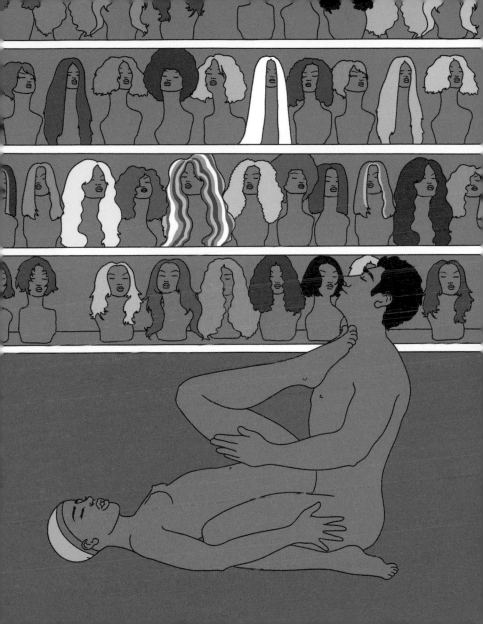

THE MANACLES

For extra enjoyment,
grind yourself on their
helpless body.

"Pin your lover in
a hold they won't
wish to fight"

THE WOMAN'S SNARE

Even a light hold controls
them; if they're a lover of
feet, this is pure heaven.

"Catch your
partner between
your feet, and
they're at your
mercy"

DAY
191

THE SHARP TILT

Every couple has their
own fit; try leaning back
and forth to test it.

"Find your most
daring angle"

DAY 192

BREATH OF PLEASURE

Before the kissing and licking begin, warm your lover until they're frantic with impatience.

"Tantalize them with the heat of your mouth"

DAY 193

THE CRAB

Enclosing your lover like this will hold their heart, as well as their body.

"A sweet, sudden embrace where the penetrated one clutches with all limbs at once"

DIVING FROM THE BRIDGE

A position to wrestle and laugh in.

"Plunge into a sweet tangle of flesh"

THE ARCHER

You can contemplate an elegant dance melting into squirming arousal.

"Stretch your lover like a bow and pluck them to climax"

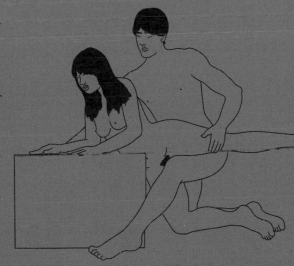

DAY 196

THE FOLDED BENCH

A fine position in which to take a few playful slaps at their lovely bottom.

"Exposed and excited, your partner's whole body is within your reach"

DAY 197 | THE RUBBING GAME

Each lover tries to tip the other while keeping their sensitive parts erotically aligned.

"Square yourselves off for a good tussle"

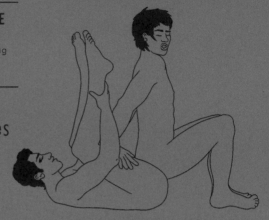

DAY 198 | THE CRANE

Parting your legs in this way allows your lover entry while you remain pleasantly tight.

"The one in front trails back a leg to open themselves to their beloved"

DAY
199

RIPPING SILK

Named for the sound the nails make, this is a thrilling yet gentle caress.

"Scrape your nails across your lover until their skin tingles in ecstasy"

DAY
200

THE DOUBLE COMPASS

Maybe best not to try
penetration in this pose,
but excellent for rubbing
together.

"Measure your pleasure
by squirming degrees"

DAY
201
THE STRADDLE

An eternally popular position in every culture.

"Make love in sweet, easy harmony"

DAY 202 | TAKING WING

Lie back on a stool or on a bed if you prefer a more restful posture.

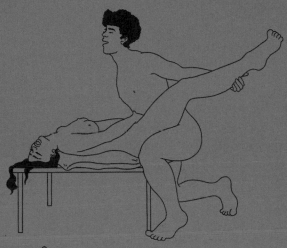

"As the penetrating partner thrusts from a crouch, they drive both lovers into flight"

DAY 203 | TWO PAINTBRUSHES

A challenge to sustain, but all the more artistic for that.

"Wet your lips and work with all your craft"

DAY
204

THE DOUBLE CLASP

A game that gives each
partner the thrill of both
the hunter and the hunted.

"Each lover grips
the other, unable to
escape and unwilling
to relinquish"

STANCE OF THE COURTESAN

There's more to lovemaking than just congress, so play on each other's desires from the outset.

"Climb down to your couch in limber playfulness"

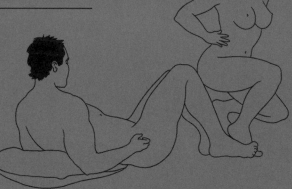

THE FOOT'S CARESS

The skin of the instep is particularly satiny—let them feel just how sleek you are.

"Trace your toes over your lover's sensitive skin"

DAY 207

THE JOLTING CART

Nicely comfortable for a rear-entry reverse, this is well worth a try.

"Bump and bounce your way to satisfaction"

DAY 208

RESTING SEAT

One in which to try flexing
your love muscles in or
around your partner.

"Meditate together
as your flesh
intermingles"

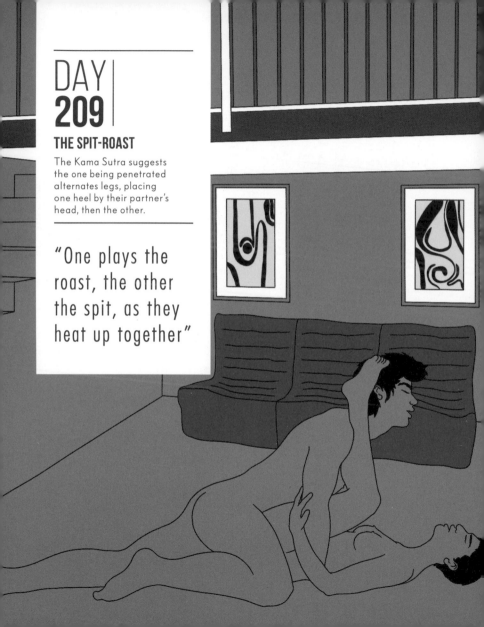

DAY 209

THE SPIT-ROAST

The Kama Sutra suggests
the one being penetrated
alternates legs, placing
one heel by their partner's
head, then the other.

"One plays the
roast, the other
the spit, as they
heat up together"

THE BLENDED KNOT

This position allows for vigorous thrusting while still feeling friendly and tender.

"Tangle yourselves tight for real passion"

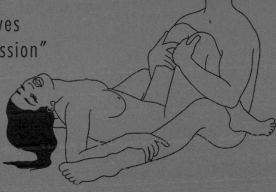

THE DEER

Thrust as your lover swings back and forth on their hands.

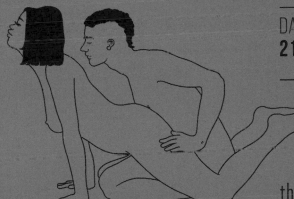

"Rut together through the wild fall nights"

DAY 212

PARIMRSHTAKA (STRIKING AT THE TIP)

A lively variation to regular sucking in which your tongue delivers hard licks against the glans.

"Flick firm against their sensitive flesh"

DAY 213 | POLISHING THE JEWEL
A loving partner attends to their lover's clitoris during congress.

"As you rock together, the motion of your thumb lights them up with desire"

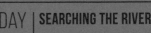

DAY 214 | SEARCHING THE RIVER
An unusual position that allows the one beneath caresses from both sides at once.

"Find their flow by touch as you press your body blindly against them"

DAY 215

THE SLEEPING CAT

A game in which one partner feigns sleep, making sure they're coyly positioned on the bed before their lover enters the room.

"Doze in perfect innocence as they creep up to pleasure you both"

DAY 216

SPLITTING THE TANGERINE

Flick your tongue teasingly between their toes before sucking them.

"Delicious pleasure for the love-hungry couple"

DAY 217

THE THUNDERBOLT

There's nothing like hard, rapid thrusts to make them cry out.

"Strike deep and electrifying"

THE LANDED ARROW

A challenging and
submissive posture for the
one lying down, calling for
strength from both lovers.

"As gravity
draws your
partner's blood
down, you work
to draw it up"

THE BAMBOO POLES

Cross and recross your
legs to roll yourself
against their hand.

"Keep sliding one
leg over another
for a slippery,
resonant rhythm"

DAY 220

LOVE'S WHEEL

This can be done with the one penetrating either sitting or kneeling—a favorite with passionate lovers.

"Rotate your hips until your partner is dizzy with desire"

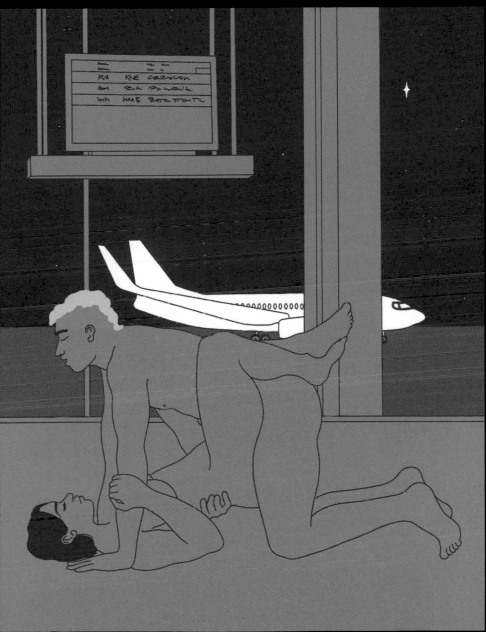

DAY 221 | THE SEE-SAW

A chance to refresh your intimacy, no matter how long you've been together.

"Enjoy the playful give-and-take of new love"

DAY 222 | THE WRESTLERS

A tussle of thighs that heightens the excitement of congress.

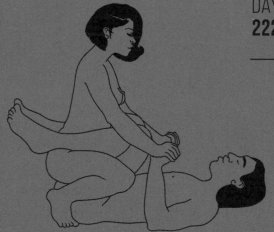

"Pit your legs against each other — until you both win"

DAY
223

WILLOW LEAVES

A position to rub together
rather than attempt
penetration, but none
the worse for that.

"Twined around
each other, the
lovers feel a flutter
of excitement"

DAY 224

THE SLANTED KISS

Sometimes it's good to get back to basics and enjoy true simplicity.

"A tilted angle for long, slow exploration"

DAY 225

THE BIRD

An easy and delightful position for the one on top to pleasure both of you at once.

"Kiss your beloved as their arousal soars"

DRAWING NEAR

Working up the sensitive insides of their thighs can leave your partner breathless and eager.

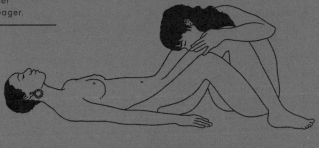

"Begin the oral pleasure far from the central prize"

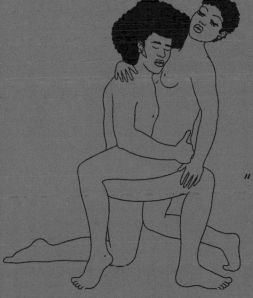

THE SUNBURST

A demanding position, especially if you attempt penetration, but good to enjoy feeling your lover's muscles strain.

"Legs spiraling out like sun rays, the couple heat each other's passion"

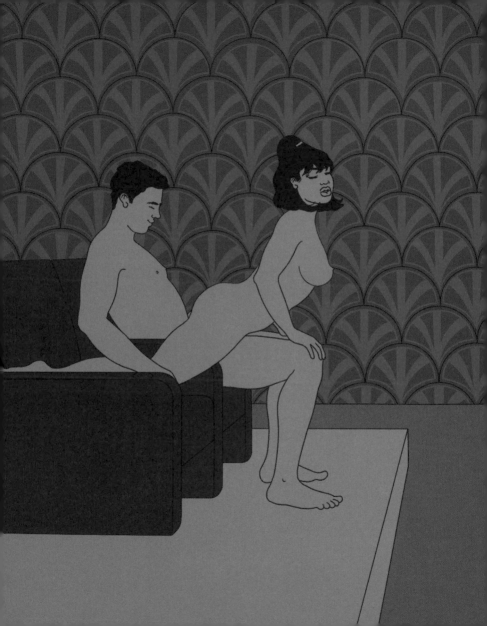

DAY 228

THE SEAL

The seated partner should take a strong hold on their lover's legs for counterbalance here.

"Rise and dive into joy"

CLIMBING THE HILL

Try this sliding against each other's oiled skin for a nonpenetrative thrill.

"Scale peaks of pleasure against your lover's body"

THE QUIVERING KISS

The Kama Sutra suggests you pinch their lips together before lavishing them with delicate kisses.

"A shivering tongue deepens tremors"

DAY | 231

QUAKING EARTH

Rising hard against your lover challenges and matches them thrust for thrust.

"Shake your lover with the strength of your hips"

DAY
232

CROSSED BRANCHES

A peaceful and affectionate pose for lovers who can share comfortable silence.

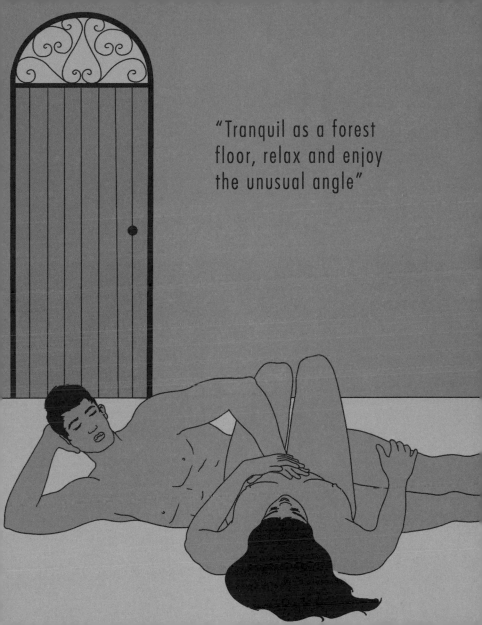

"Tranquil as a forest floor, relax and enjoy the unusual angle"

DAY
233

THE MELTING EMBRACE

A warm, cozy, full-body caress for tender moments.

"Rest together and let your sensations merge"

DAY 234 | THE JUGGLER
To achieve this, begin with a handstand, then lean back as your partner holds you.

"Bring out your inner circus star"

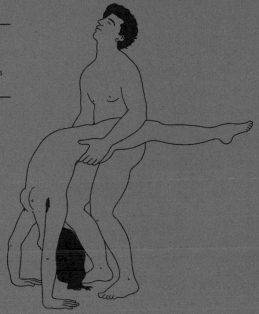

DAY 235 | THE SURPRISE
A game only for lovers long acquainted—ask in advance if they like the idea.

"Waken your beloved by gently entering their body"

DAY
236

NUDGING OPEN

A skilled lover can coax their partner's legs apart with hand and penis working together.

"A tantalizing approach from behind when the penetrated partner cannot go forward"

THE TONGUE MASSAGE

The Kama Sutra recommends the lover "worship vigorously" here.

"Enter their archway with the tip of your tongue before licking deep"

THE RIVER MEETS THE SEA

A position where the one in front controls most of the movement, as the penetrating partner's legs hold their hips still.

"Flow into their undulating depths"

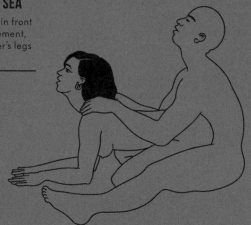

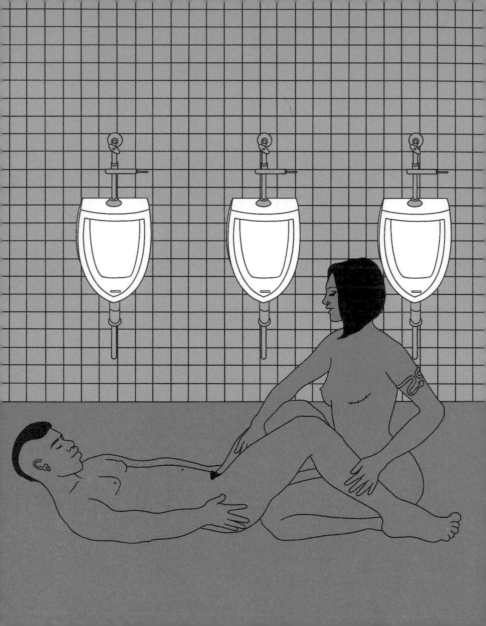

DAY
240
FINGER WALK

A sensual tickle for those who know how to make their partner wait.

"Dance up toward their penis — then teasingly away"

DAY 241

THE CROSSED KNIVES

More a sexercise than a
position for penetration,
but excellent for foreplay.

"Rise together
to sharpen up
your appetites"

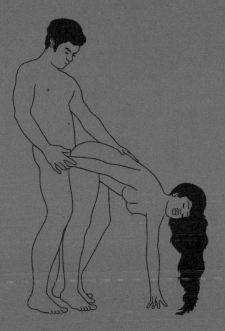

DAY 242 | CONGRESS OF A COW

A Kama Sutra classic—testing for the legs but wonderful for deep penetration.

"True animal joy for the unashamedly lusty"

DAY 243 | OILING THE GATES

Those lovely thighs stretch and strain in many positions, some care lavished on them can make all the difference.

"Prepare them for a challenge with some soft work"

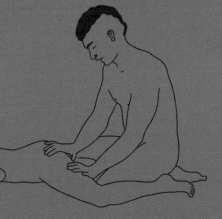

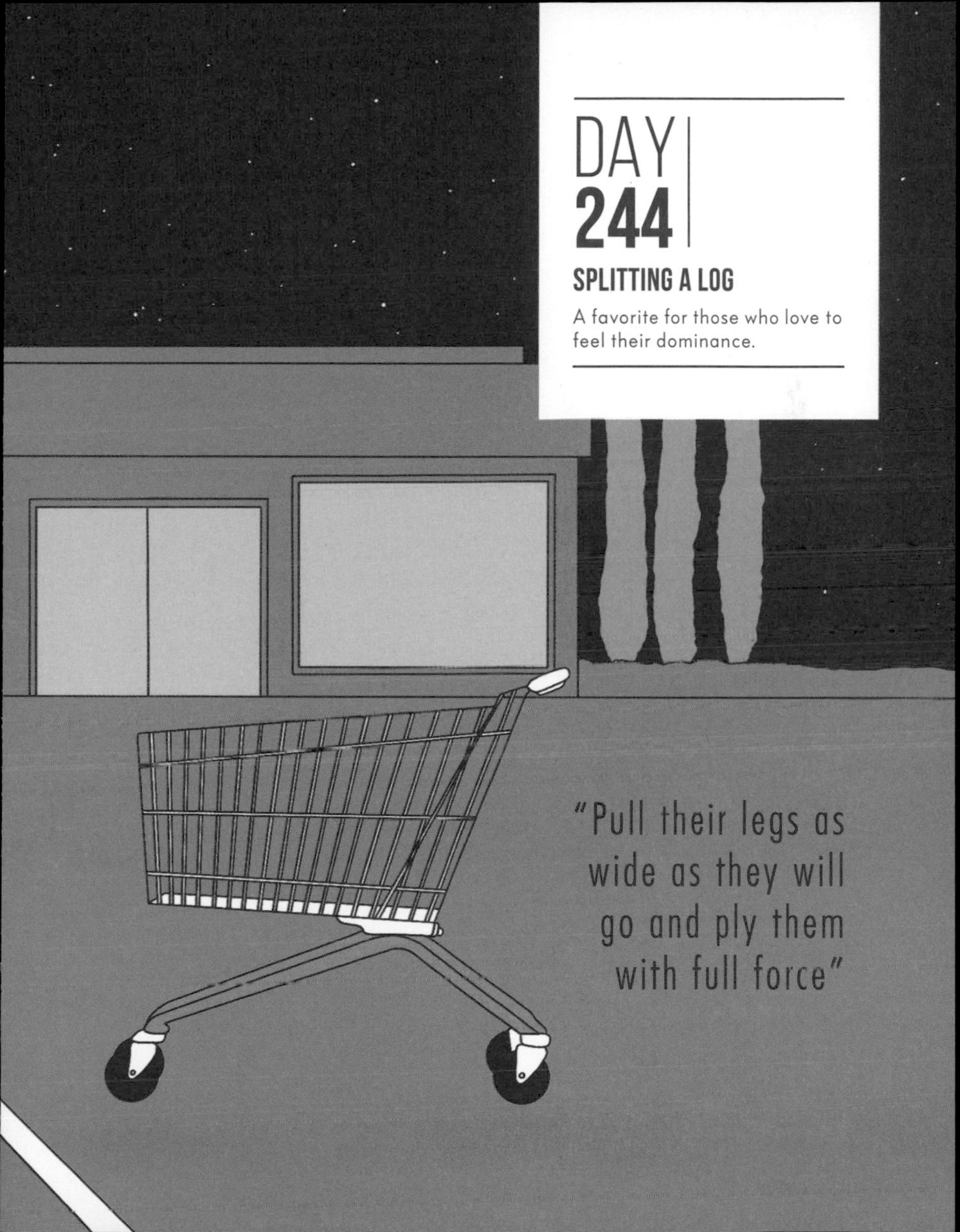

DAY 244

SPLITTING A LOG

A favorite for those who love to feel their dominance.

"Pull their legs as wide as they will go and ply them with full force"

DAY
245
THE SILENT REQUEST
A guessing game for lovers, with only the movement of your mouth to clue them in as to what you want next.

"Shape the words against their waiting lips"

DAY
246
THE KNOT OF FLAME
The Panchasayaka says that in this position, the loins leap together with a sound like the flapping of elephant ears!

"Pull each other close in burning passion"

DAY
247

THE FLOATING CANES

Your legs hang in the
air and your body rocks
with the motion of your
partner's thrusts.

"Drift away into
deep delight"

DAY
248

THE GAZING MEDITATION
The power of an unbroken glance can't be understated: spend five full minutes moving each other wordlessly.

"Don't speak — just let your expressions dance together"

DAY
249

THE DROPPED HEAD

For an extra thrill, hang your head low enough that your breathing constricts—as long as your partner minds your safety.

"A rush of blood dizzies and excites"

DAY 250 | THE HALF-TURN

A position to surprise and confuse our expectations, charming for playful moments.

"Keep yourselves in suspense"

DAY 251 | RAISING THE HAMMOCK

For those who love to glory in their strength, this is a position to boast of.

"Give in to absolute helplessness as your lover hoists"

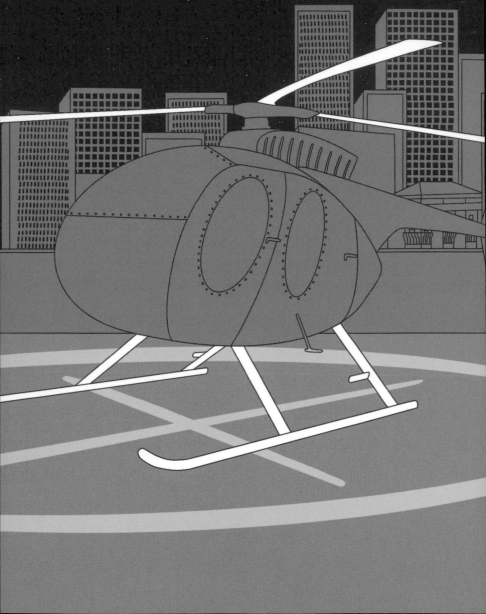

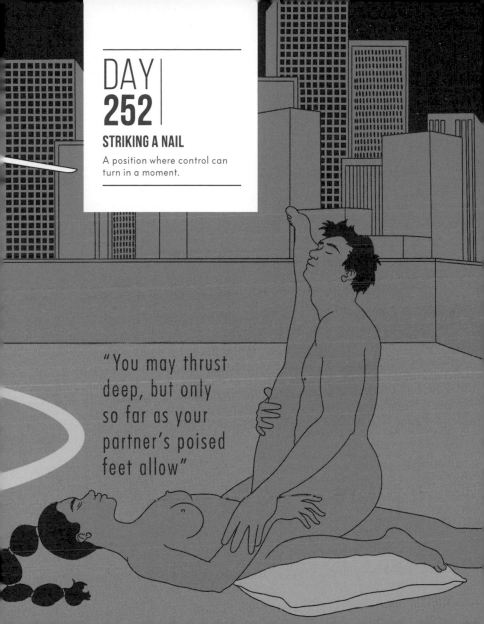

DAY | 252

STRIKING A NAIL

A position where control can turn in a moment.

"You may thrust deep, but only so far as your partner's poised feet allow"

DAY 253 | THE SHALLOW OCEAN

Penetration here can depend on the couple having compatibly angled genitals, but it's lovely as an embrace, too.

"Let pleasure lap you as you ebb and flow together"

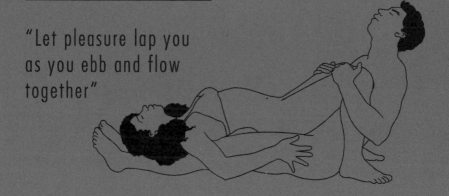

DAY 254 | THE SPIDER CARESS

Rake your nails very gently across their sensitive scalp— the resulting chills can be surprisingly intense.

"Send shivers down their spine"

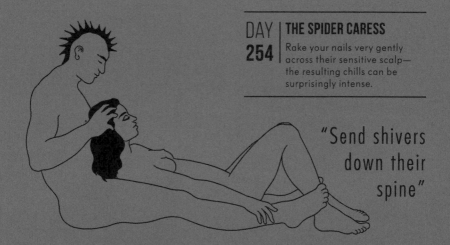

DAY | 255

THE STROKING STOMACH

A wonderful double delight:
the pleasure of your touch
and the sight of your graceful
movements.

"Rub back and
forth on your
partner's member
until they gasp
with desire"

DAY 256

THE BUTTERFLY EMBRACE

The contrast between the light fingers and warm pressing of hips can be delectable.

"Trace delicate patterns of beauty across each other's backs"

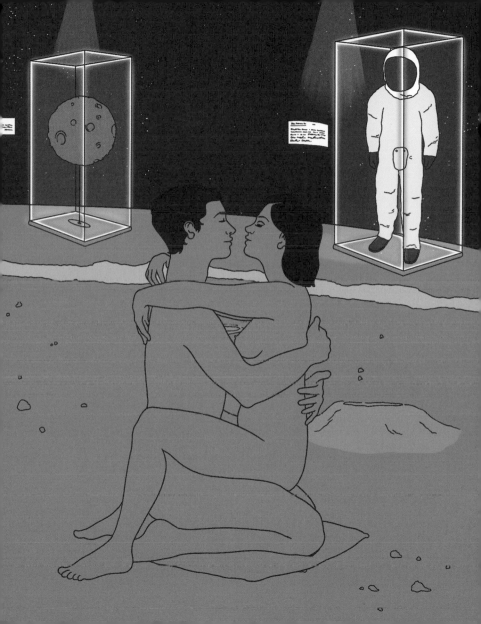

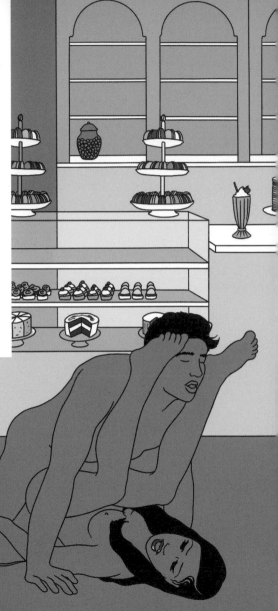

DAY 257

THE BUFFET

A thrust the Kama Sutra describes as a complete withdrawal followed by a deep strike to the womb.

"A swift, hard in-and-out that draws a cry from the most languid lover"

DAY 258 | THE ALTAR

One for the gymnasts, but a fine feat if you can manage it.

"One partner extends themselves to play sacrifice for their beloved"

DAY 259 | THE DEEP PRESS

Leaning back, the one on top rests their weight on their lover's shoulders for an extra thrill.

"Squeeze them breathless within and without"

DAY
260
THE ACORN

A useful rear-entry position
for creating a tight grip.

"Tucked tight,
ready for great
pleasure to grow"

THE GROOMING CAT

A good way to get an unusual angle and an extra pleasure for those who love their partner's legs.

"Lift up a leg like a purring puss and let your lover's energy refresh you"

PIDITAKA (PRESSING)

A love stroke the Kama Sutra suggests for variety; if your partner is shallow inside, be gentle.

"Sink in and push to the very depths"

DAY 263

ROCKING THE CANOE

For the less athletic, add the support of a stool or two.

"Rise and fall on a gentle current"

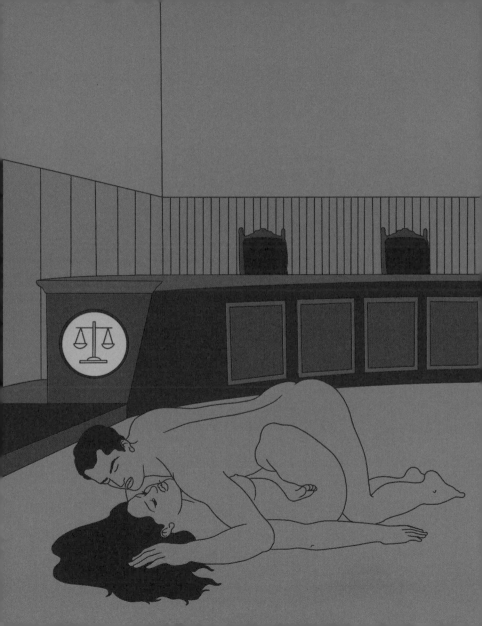

DAY 264

THE LOTUS

The Lotus—the penetrated partner's legs crossed one above another—is one of the Kama Sutra's most famous positions.

"A yummy, yogic classic"

DAY
265
THE SWING

An energetic rise-and-fall game to stimulate the body.

"Secure your limbs together and rock, as carefree as children"

DAY
266

THE PRANCING DOE

An embrace that can become passionate lovemaking in an instant.

"Leap against your stag's body"

DAY
267

THE BULL'S HORNS

A comfortable position for those who are ready to surrender.

"Bend your proud lover to your will"

DAY
268
THE HALF-MOUNT

A fun variation to liven up
more conventional sex.

"Twist to cast a
flirtatious glance
even in congress"

DAY 269 | THE QUEEN'S GREETING

A mischievous way to start the seduction—give them a royal surprise.

"Enthrone yourself unexpectedly"

DAY 270 | FLOATING CONGRESS

A couple in which one is strong and the other small works best for this.

"Wrapped in beauty, you'll know delight from head to foot"

DAY 271

THE MONKEY

A natural position with a twisting thrust, bringing out the primal self.

"Rotate within the cave of their thighs until they cry aloud"

DAY 272

THE HALF-SQUEEZE

Pulling you closer, your partner is penetrated to the core.

"Enclosed but moving freely, you can thrust with all your vitality"

DAY 273

THE COILED MOUNT

There's nothing like a firm inner grip, so roll yourself into a ball and see what happens.

"Tuck right up to give your lover a tight squeeze"

THE HARE

With steady furniture, the one penetrating can put real vigor into this.

"Nest down on a table and feel the joys of spring"

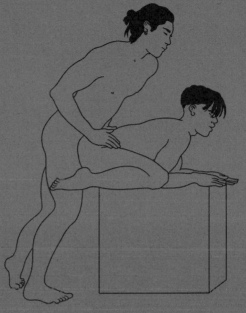

THE SWAN'S EMBRACE

A sensual way to cuddle up for long, sweet kisses.

"Shelter between your partner's legs and whisper together"

DAY 276

THE FAN

By bracing their arms both backward and forward, the one on top can steady themselves for long thrusts.

"Sweep back and forth until you both flutter into climax"

TWO FROGS

An energetic
position, but be
careful not to
slip apart.

"Powered by your
thrusting legs,
leap joyfully
together"

THE SCABBARD

One to make you feel
like a true warrior.

"Cast aside your
inhibitions and
slip right into
each other"

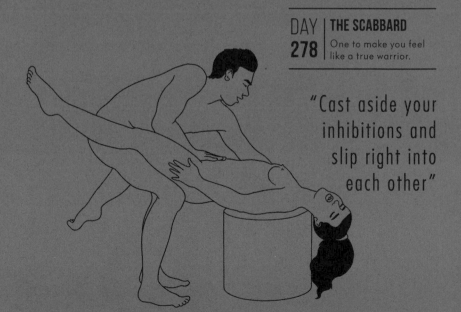

DAY 279

CRUSHING THE SPICES

The trick is to revolve from facing their head to their feet without slipping apart.

"Sweeten the moment with a careful turn south"

DAY
280

CROSSING THE
HIGHER PATH

For lovers looking
to woo gently, this is
an enchanting way
to begin.

"A line of delicate kisses
across their collarbone"

DAY
281

THE BRANCH IN BLOSSOM

A fine position to lie back and
luxuriate in the balmy moment.

"Sway as in a
gentle breeze"

DAY | **THE OPEN DOOR**
282 | A stable and comfortable variant on the wide-open poses.

"Enter your beloved freely"

DAY | **THE BREATHING THRONE**
283 | A challenge to the muscles that wakes up the whole body.

"Each lover opens their lungs and inhales in the dizzy moment"

DAY | 284

THE TRAPEZE

As long as your grip holds out, you free your partner to put all their energy into thrusting.

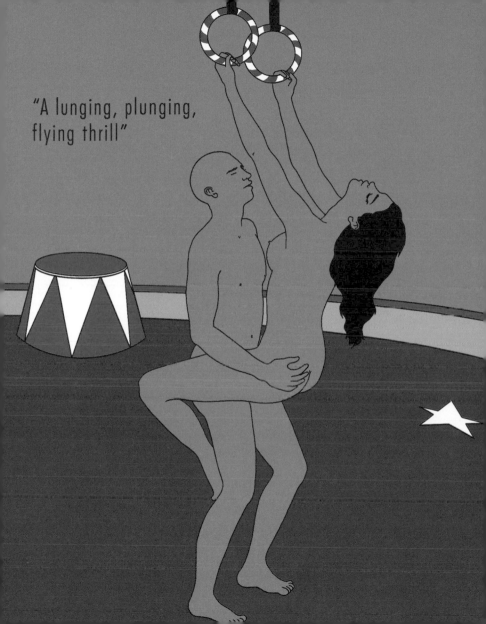

"A lunging, plunging, flying thrill"

THE LIZARD
A good position for
lovers' talk and teasing.

"Creep across your
resting lover with a
sensuous slither"

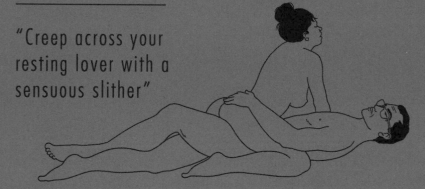

THE TIGRESS'S TAIL
Twine a leg back and
stroke your lover's back.

"An unexpected
tickle for the
tiger"

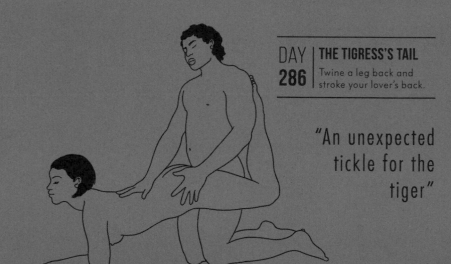

DAY
287

PLUCKING THE LUTE

The thoughtful lover tends
to their partner's clitoris
with a musician's skill.

"Play a double
chord of pleasure"

DAY 288

THROWING THE CLAY

A passionate tumble allowing
a change of positions midflow.

"Cast them down
and mold their
limbs to yours"

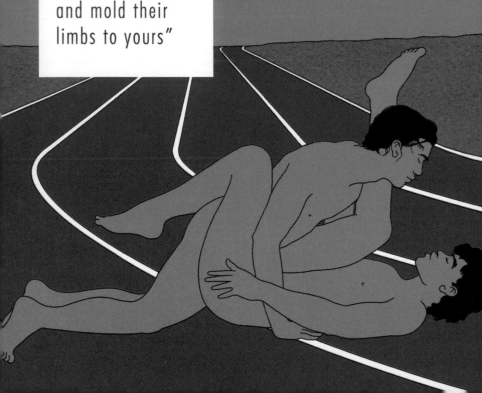

DAY
289
THE SHOULDER STOOL

This requires acrobatic ability, but there's a lot of fun to be had in trying.

"Profound abandon for the one penetrating as their partner balances"

THE OPEN BOOK

Make love without
speaking, with only
your senses for a guide.

"Let your body be
a lesson for your
lover to read"

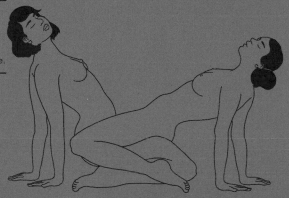

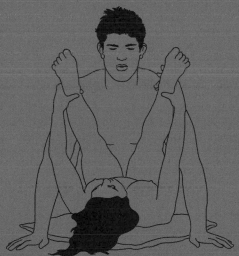

THE BULL'S BLOW

The Kama Sutra describes
this thrust as "like a bull
tossing his horns."

"Strike wildly in
all directions"

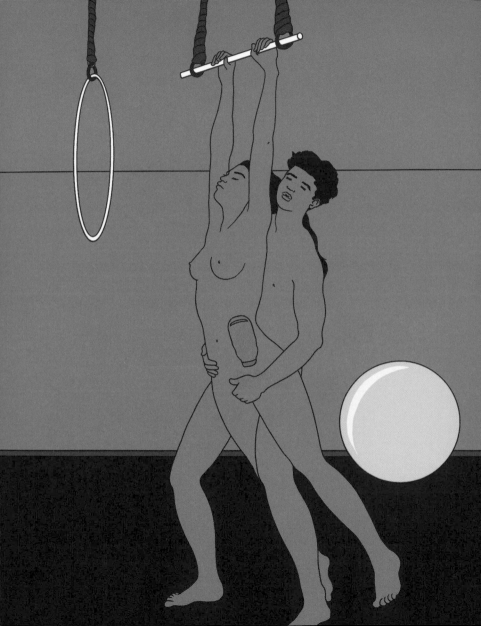

DAY
292

GREETING THE MOON

A delectable embrace to
whet the appetite.

"Stretch to the
sky while their
fingers stray to
the depths"

DAY 293 | THE LIONESS SUPPORTED
Propping yourselves up in this position lets you think of nothing but each other.

"Let a stool take the weight off your minds"

DAY 294 | THE BOAR'S BLOW
The Kama Sutra defines this as continuous pressure on one side of the yoni.

"Single-minded satisfaction"

DAY 295

LOVE'S ARROW

The Ratikallolini suggests raising one foot to your own heart, but your partner's chest is just as good for those who are less flexible.

"Let yourself be pierced with pleasure"

"The lightest touch can be the sweetest"

DAY
296

FEATHER FINGERS

Stroke ever so gently up and down your beloved's skin.

DAY 297

ROCKING THE TURTLE

The one on top trusts their balance entirely to their lover and thinks only of their desire.

"Come out of your shell ... or let them into yours"

DAY
298

HOLDING THE BOW

More of an embrace than a sex position, but wonderful to show off your physique.

"Stretch your body taut for your partner's excitement"

DAY
299

LOVE'S DART ANTICIPATED

A position to hold and wait until the temptation grows too hard to resist.

"Tantalize yourselves with their rising penis"

DAY 300

THE CLIMBING MONKEY

A position that needs a willowy penetrated partner, but tremendous fun if it suits your body type.

"Scamper into reckless mischief"

HALF-WRAPPED

A great deep-entry
position that's not too
limb-bendingly yogic.

"Enclose your
lover with a single,
sinuous limb"

THE COURTESAN'S GAMBIT

A gymnastic position that
allows each lover to focus on
their own excitement.

"Pleasure
yourself openly
as they thrust"

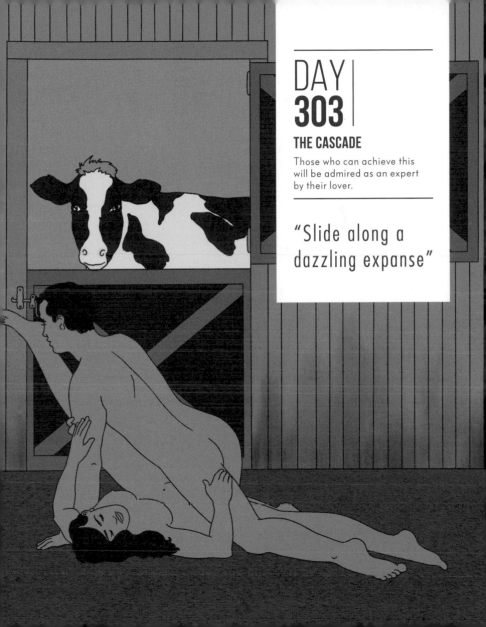

DAY
303

THE CASCADE

Those who can achieve this will be admired as an expert by their lover.

"Slide along a dazzling expanse"

DAY
304

THE RIVER DOLPHIN

A pose the one on top can assume for relaxation during lovemaking.

"Rise for breath amid the flow of your ecstasy"

DAY 305

THE LITTER BEARER

A strain on all but the mightiest of thighs, but you can always move to a chair if your partner tires.

"Your lover is absolutely at your service"

DAY
306

THE KIDNAPPER'S HOLD
A fun way to grab your
partner's attention and
start a sexy game.

"Steal them away
from routine"

DAY
307

THE QUEST
Undoubtedly not the
easiest angle, but a
lot of fun can be had
in the attempt.

"Find your way
and win true
glory!"

DAY
308

THE MIRROR DANCE

A charming game to
deepen intimacy.

"Meld together
and move in
perfect harmony"

PROFFERING

A tender-hearted lover can please their partner with their hand at the same time.

"Lift and lay open your whole body for your beloved"

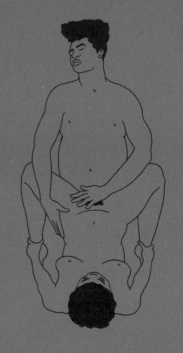

BEAUTY TENDED

A loving and relaxing position for those times when they deserve all your attention.

"Hold your lover safe for the journey into climax"

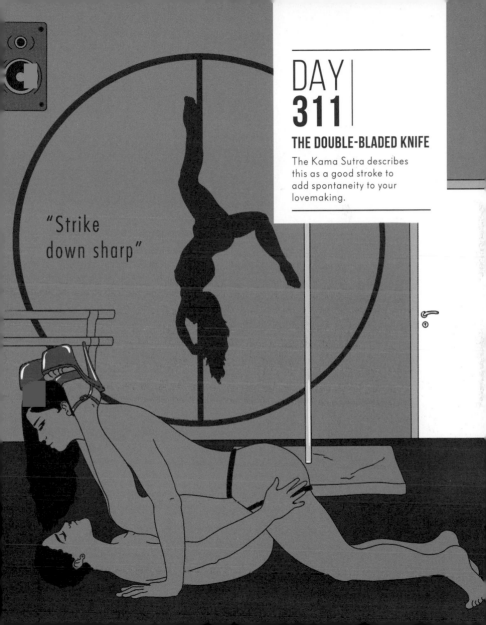

DAY 311

THE DOUBLE-BLADED KNIFE

The Kama Sutra describes this as a good stroke to add spontaneity to your lovemaking.

"Strike down sharp"

DAY 312

THE BED WITH NO SHEETS

Unwise to attempt penetration here, but fine for waking up the vigor and impressing your partner.

"Raise yourself up to be your beloved's couch"

DAY
313

THE THIGH'S TREASURE

With some lubrication, this is a sweet treat for those days when you don't want penetration.

"No one will forget the silken delights of their lover's skin"

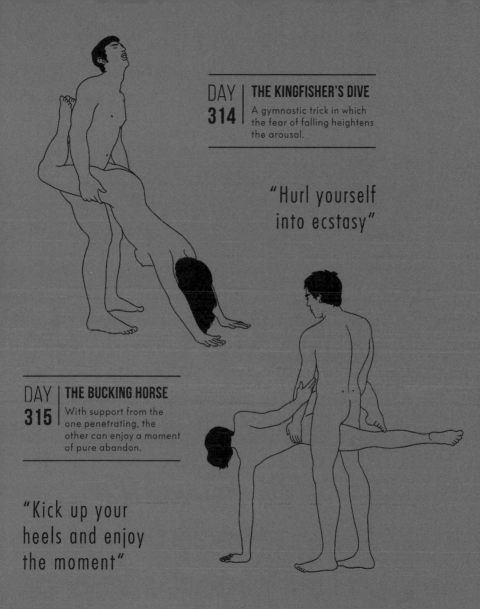

DAY
314 | **THE KINGFISHER'S DIVE**
A gymnastic trick in which the fear of falling heightens the arousal.

"Hurl yourself into ecstasy"

DAY
315 | **THE BUCKING HORSE**
With support from the one penetrating, the other can enjoy a moment of pure abandon.

"Kick up your heels and enjoy the moment"

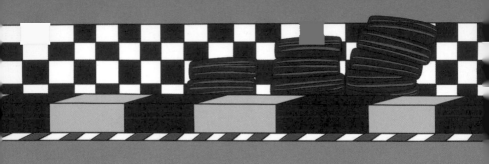

DAY
316

THE DOUBLE CROUCH

A bouncy position that lets each partner contribute some flexible fun.

"Grind and grin with your legs all twined together"

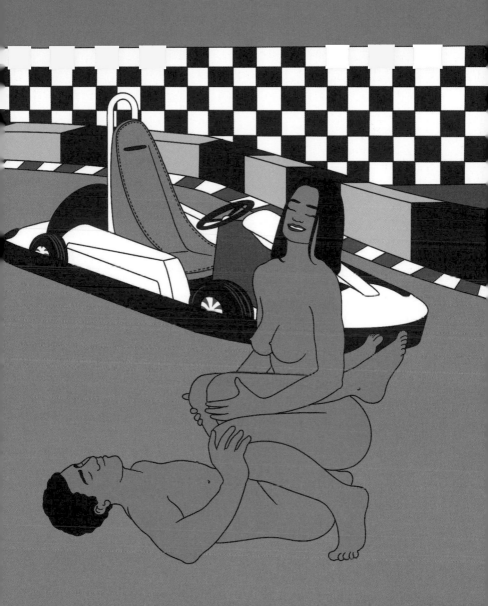

THE CASTING EMBRACE

A passionate move to sweep
them off their feet.

"Throw your partner
back in your arms and
shower burning kisses
on their chest"

PEEPING UNDER THE GATE

If you can't achieve penetration
in this position, you can still enjoy
the slippery fun of it.

"Meet each
other's gaze in
an unexpected
intimacy"

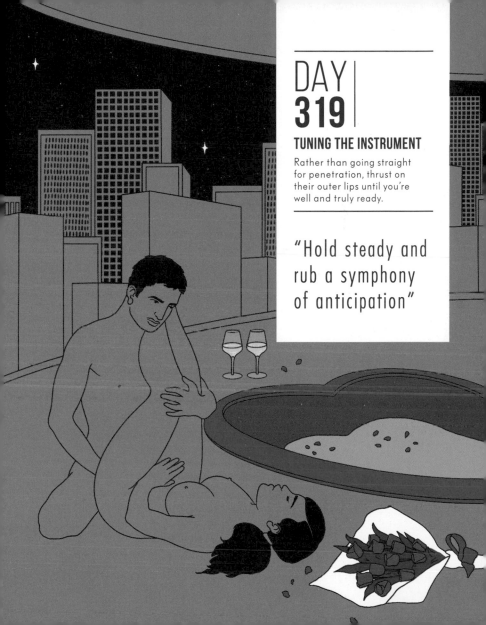

DAY 319

TUNING THE INSTRUMENT

Rather than going straight for penetration, thrust on their outer lips until you're well and truly ready.

"Hold steady and rub a symphony of anticipation"

THE FALLING BRANCH

A sensuous way to change
positions and move into a
new embrace.

"Sink with a sigh as
they admire your
flowering beauty"

DAY 321

EQUAL FEET

The Ratikallolini calls this position a way to ecstasy.

"Caress your partner with your feet and hands working in harmony"

THE LOVER'S NOOSE

A device most charming,
according to the
Smaradipika.

"Press your thighs
around them so hard
they gasp"

THE STRIDE

A sensuous way to start
the love-play.

"Lean up against
your lover and
slide happily"

DAY
324

THE SOLDIER'S EMBRACE

An energetic position, useful
for when you just have to have
each other right now.

"Grab your chance,
bed or not"

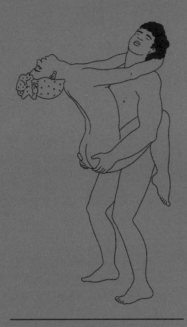

CARRYING THE BASKET

You can be supported with
a table if need be, but it's
fun to try free-standing.

"Bounce in your
lover's arms, a
merry burden"

THE INVISIBLE TRAP

A good trick to play, leaving
the one penetrating free to
control from below.

"With your legs tilting
your partner, they
must move at your
chosen pace"

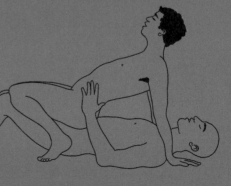

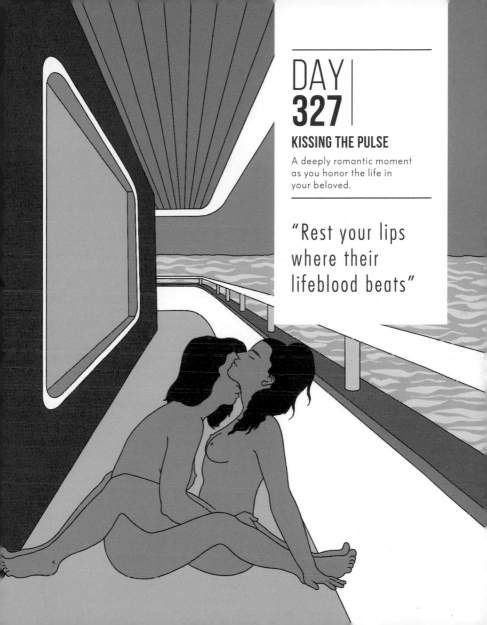

DAY | 327

KISSING THE PULSE

A deeply romantic moment as you honor the life in your beloved.

"Rest your lips where their lifeblood beats"

DAY
328

MOSS ON A BRANCH

An elastic and
intimate embrace for
meditative moments.

"Cling close and let
your intimacy grow"

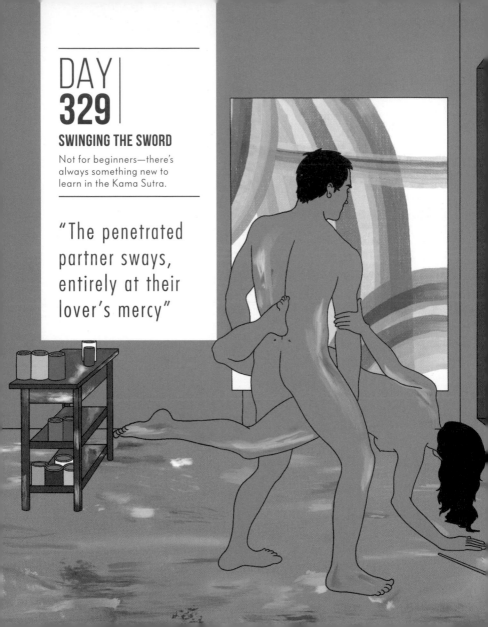

DAY 329

SWINGING THE SWORD

Not for beginners—there's always something new to learn in the Kama Sutra.

"The penetrated partner sways, entirely at their lover's mercy"

DAY
330

THE TEST OF TRUST

Show your love by balancing your desire to caress with your pledge to keep them safe.

"Please your partner, but keep them from falling"

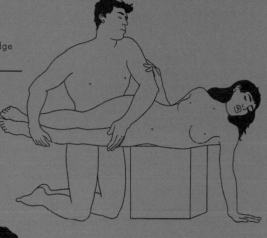

DAY
331

TWO TREES GROWING TOGETHER

A passionate position, calling for the lovers to combine their strength.

"Rise from the bed as one"

DAY
332

THE SUMMONING WIND

A teasing, tingly way to begin
your seduction.

"Call your
beloved from
rest with a
playful breeze"

THE LEAPING OTTER

A playful and challenging position, best tried over a soft surface.

"Get ready to be submerged in pleasure"

THE TURNAROUND

A highly accomplished trick that must be learned with careful practice.

"Show yourselves limber enough to rotate without losing the connection"

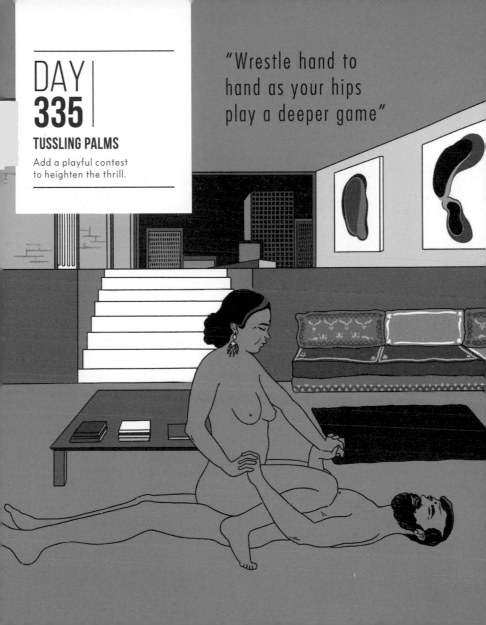

DAY 335

TUSSLING PALMS

Add a playful contest
to heighten the thrill.

"Wrestle hand to
hand as your hips
play a deeper game"

DAY
336
THE LOWERED LOTUS

The Kama Sutra suggests the one being penetrated crosses their legs under their partner's chin, but this is an easier variant for most people.

"Wind yourself in comfort around your lover's strong flanks"

DAY | 337

THE CLINGING CREEPER

A slow, gentle twining the Ratimanjari compares to the sway of the fragrant jasmine plant.

"Their limbs rise and fall to the rhythm of your thrusting"

DAY
338

DRAWING THE HEARTBEAT

A tender, tantalizing caress for lovers prolonging the anticipation.

"Trace a fingertip for their love to follow"

DAY
339

THE BASKET OF SCARVES

Get nice and twisted together until you're hardly sure whose body is whose.

"Wind your limbs in tangling confusion"

DAY 340

THE STAIRCASE SEIZED

Bending one leg all the way up helps make use of the limited space.

"Sometimes the bedroom is just too far away"

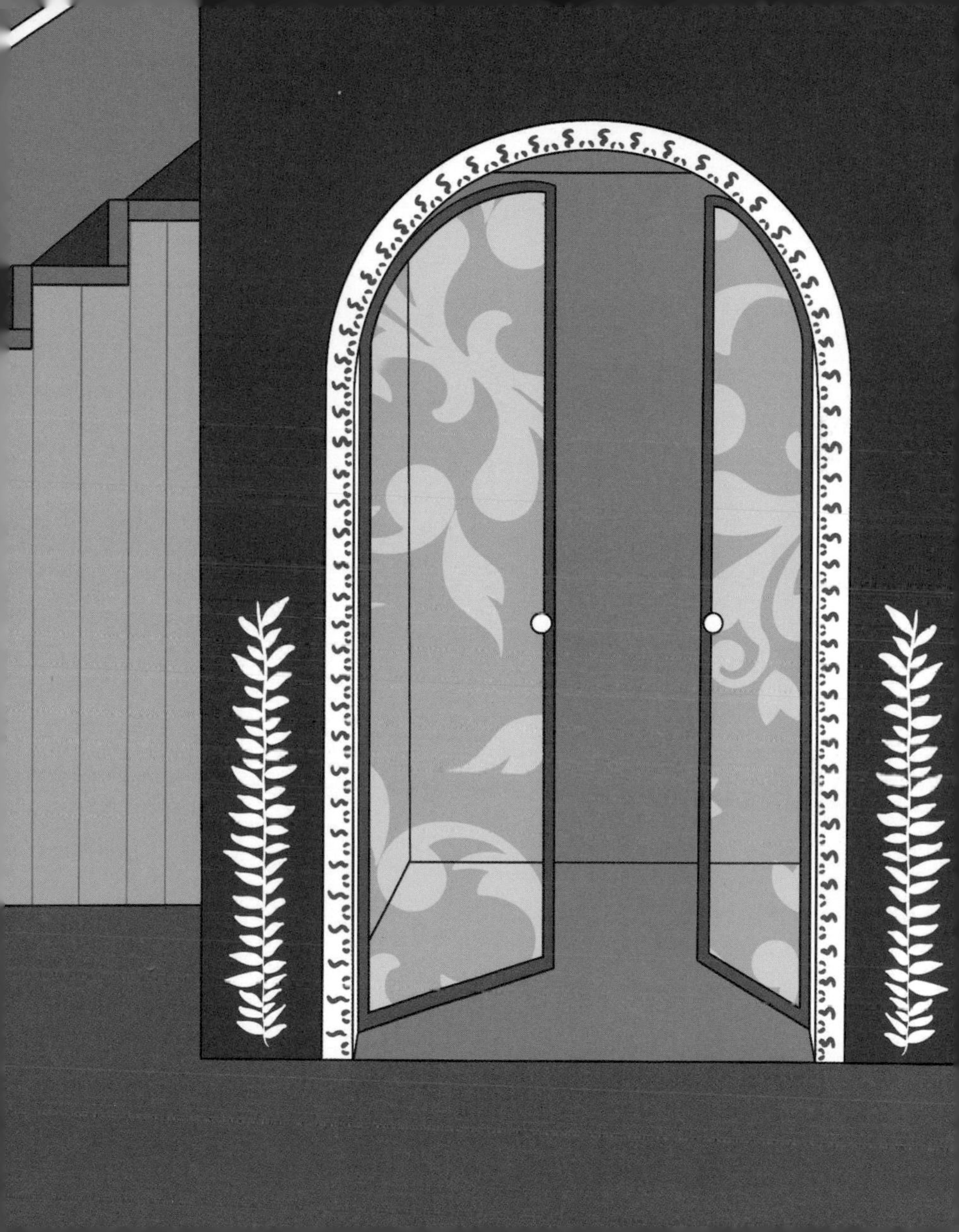

THE BREATHING PULSE

A sexual meditation that combines vigorous movement and intense self-awareness.

"Thrust and breathe together in perfect unison"

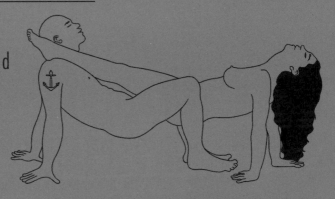

THE STRIDING FOX

If the one being penetrated can maintain their position, this is surprisingly comfortable for the other partner.

"Make a wild territory of your bed"

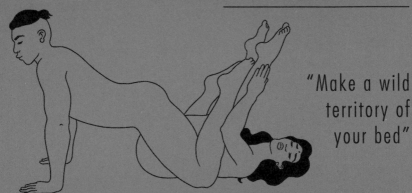

DAY | 343

THE FROG

A gymnastic pose where
the bounce is half the fun.

"Spring and
swing, but don't
let them slip away"

DAY
344

THE ENCLOSED EMBRACE

Press close up against each
other's naked skin.

"Make a tight space
of your tenderness"

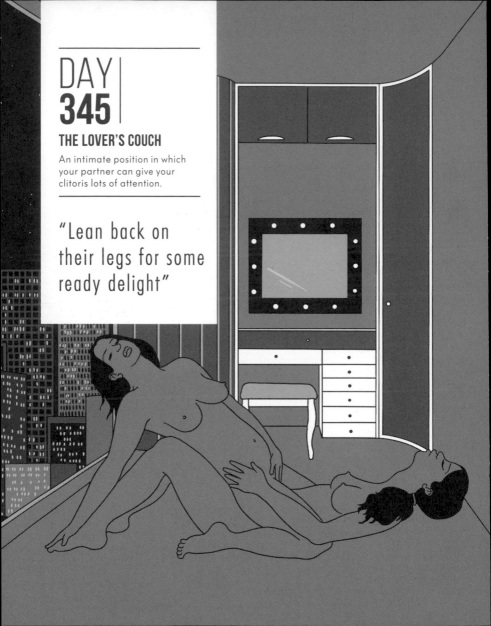

DAY 345

THE LOVER'S COUCH

An intimate position in which
your partner can give your
clitoris lots of attention.

"Lean back on
their legs for some
ready delight"

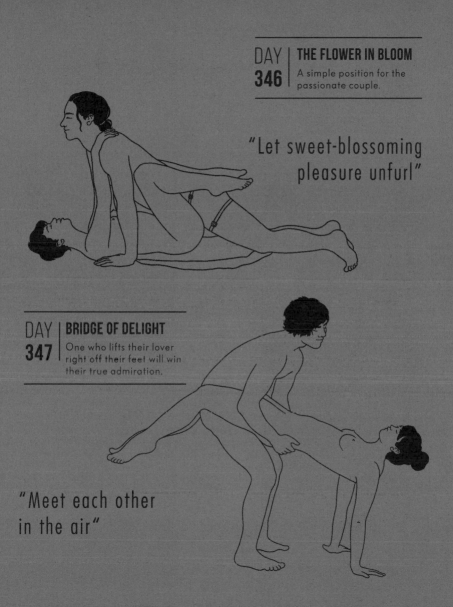

THE FLOWER IN BLOOM
A simple position for the passionate couple.

"Let sweet-blossoming pleasure unfurl"

BRIDGE OF DELIGHT
One who lifts their lover right off their feet will win their true admiration.

"Meet each other in the air"

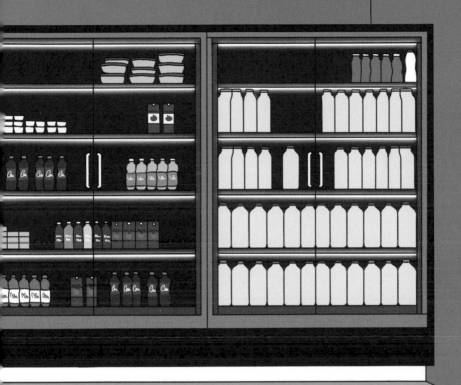

DAY 348

PLAYING THE TABLA

Lift some of your weight off your partner as you pull back for another thrust.

"Drum a rhythm on your beloved with hands and hips"

THE WATERFALL

An unusual chance to experience upside-down delights.

"Tumble into a flurry of passion"

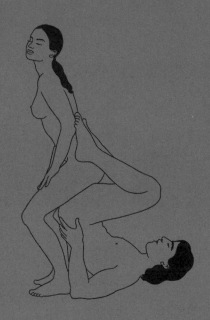

CUTTING THE ORANGE

The unusual feeling of sideways entry can refresh even a familiar passion.

"Split open their legs and dig in deep"

DAY | 351
THE MAN SURRENDERED

This can be done on a bed for comfort, but a stool increases the suspense.

"Spread and balanced, they must await their partner's pleasure"

DAY 352

THE LIGHT RIDE

The angle makes deep penetration almost impossible, forcing the couple to partake of daintier stimulation.

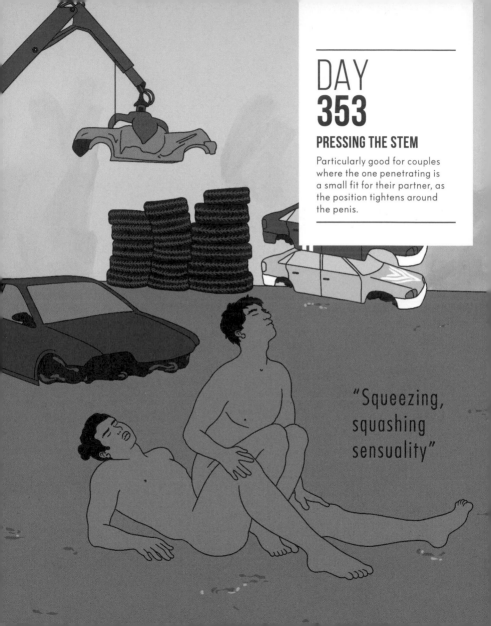

DAY
353

PRESSING THE STEM

Particularly good for couples where the one penetrating is a small fit for their partner, as the position tightens around the penis.

"Squeezing, squashing sensuality"

| **IVY AND PASSIONFRUIT**
Fit your limbs together in a perfect interlace.

"Rise together,
inextricably entwined"

| **PIERCING THE MOON**
Risky if you slip, so do it over a soft surface.

"A graceful
crescent struck
by your arrow"

DAY
356

THE THIGH'S OPPOSITION

A tease for the one lying
down—their partner ignores
their arousal and rubs
against their muscular leg.

"Make them wait
for your pleasure"

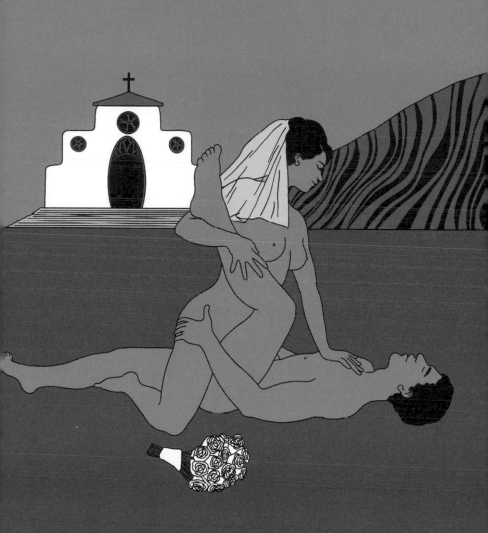

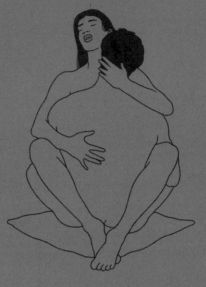

DAY 357 | THE SEATED BUD
An affectionate position for couples deeply in love.

"Pleasure them until their limbs uncurl"

DAY 358 | GRINDING THE GRAIN
With your lover comfortable on their back, you can move their hips easily.

"Bend and rotate their hips for delicious depths"

DAY 359

RIDING THE FALLEN

For those who like to take control, this is a great way to put them at your mercy.

"Your partner lies helpless as you enjoy them"

THE HALF-GENUFLECTION

With one knee poised and one
leg braced, you can thrust with
all your energy.

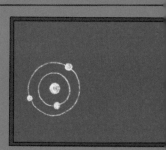

"Kneel at their shrine
for a blissful blessing"

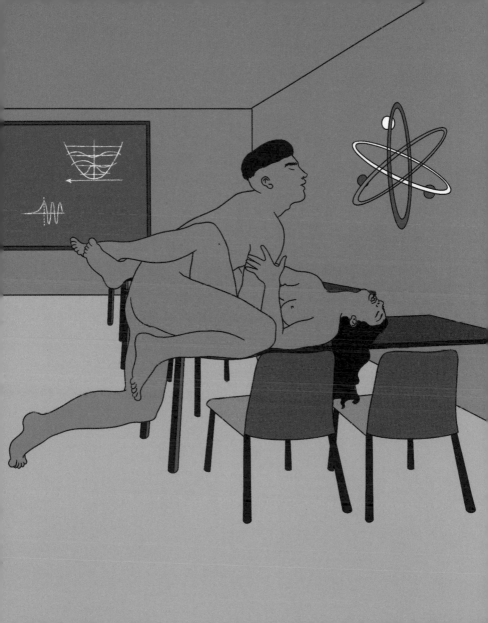

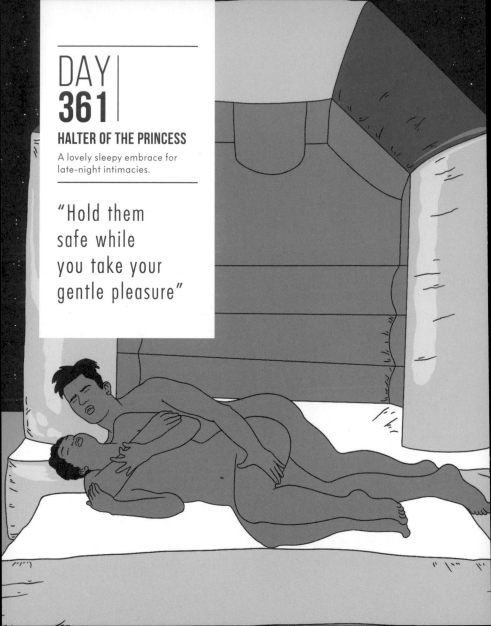

DAY 361

HALTER OF THE PRINCESS

A lovely sleepy embrace for late-night intimacies.

"Hold them safe while you take your gentle pleasure"

DAY **362** | **PLEASURE'S CHALLENGE**
A thrilling game that leads to wilder lovemaking.

"Their fingers fondle you until you fall"

DAY **363** | **THE RECKLESS GRASP**
A wild embrace for passionate reunions.

"Forget everything but the drama of your bodies"

DAY
364

THE MAIDEN'S GRANDEUR

The wide-set posture
makes your back rise
straight and haughty.

"Bring all your
pride to this
graceful seat"

DAY 365

THE SITTING SIGH

Make love, pleasure them with your hands, or just cuddle happily.

"Relax into your beloved in absolute safety"

IN THE MOOD FOR...
TRUE TENDERNESS

006	320	016	075	275	178	111	013	224
173	126	332	089	002	290	122	310	321
337	051	096	081	183	054	304	085	243
136	210	344	169	216	137	346	069	285
001	256	035	233	093	225	023	280	017
327	103	357	067	154	248	338	094	127
143	076	308	130	245	124	042	076	296
044	184	018	223	004	319	193	254	174

IN THE MOOD FOR...
DEEP ABANDON

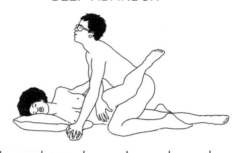

204	060	039	128	249	009	116	138	244
012	271	180	336	024	228	123	079	018
301	083	231	107	358	090	252	223	359
177	220	003	274	155	217	020	237	147
350	118	066	202	049	259	186	105	091
021	242	311	061	358	112	272	247	063
257	007	121	291	179	125	059	172	309
036	246	198	171	005	145	209	008	157

IN THE MOOD FOR...
PLAYFUL MOMENTS

046	206	114	316	027	245	149	285	009
339	008	269	056	240	190	084	045	335
010	225	140	356	194	014	265	080	158
250	176	034	170	098	348	077	142	295
197	087	298	365	323	205	007	222	115
306	160	019	333	181	127	362	072	307
028	057	286	131	043	352	106	268	022
189	006	199	074	215	016	292	141	241

IN THE MOOD FOR ...
ADVANCED ECSTASIES

032	288	209	025	324	194	062	223	214
153	134	070	353	166	050	262	133	099
258	086	347	144	082	294	119	015	270
014	322	120	364	360	211	341	317	195
351	003	191	315	187	101	222	125	349
102	095	334	133	004	325	052	302	156
227	290	168	068	309	182	264	073	229
058	219	026	151	116	012	139	255	038

IN THE MOOD FOR...
PEACEFUL EMBRACES

008	299	235	075	282	041	313	276	069
328	013	339	212	162	193	011	183	233
230	361	304	005	264	253	104	226	298
354	165	092	239	310	055	190	365	017
031	285	317	280	100	225	113	088	344
345	002	201	129	232	081	246	293	236
161	327	275	047	268	256	065	332	308
266	053	110	281	001	146	287	030	213

IN THE MOOD FOR...
UNCOMMON PLEASURES

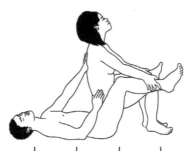

108	260	238	064	283	175	331	029	251
284	011	326	278	203	292	200	263	164
159	342	188	135	340	40	347	148	091
300	078	297	080	185	303	221	318	218
234	330	048	267	315	097	343	117	312
355	150	314	196	163	329	071	277	229
033	279	273	363	010	261	207	305	015
262	228	167	037	259	109	289	152	183

ACKNOWLEDGMENTS

ILLUSTRATOR'S ACKNOWLEDGMENTS
To my mother, Gloria, my best friend. Thank you for teaching me not to give up. I wouldn't be here without your unconditional love.

PUBLISHER'S ACKNOWLEDGMENTS
DK would like to thank Charlotte Beauchamp for editorial assistance. From the first edition: special thanks to Kesta Desmond.

ABOUT THE ILLUSTRATOR
Alicia Rihko is a freelance illustrator and designer based in Spain. She has built a strong social media following with her strikingly original erotic artworks, inspired by pop culture motifs and full of color, sensuality, and rebellious fun. Her Instagram is @aliciarihko.

Editor Megan Lea
US Editor Kayla Dugger
Designer Natalie Clay
Project Designer Louise Brigenshaw
Design Manager Marianne Markham
Managing Editor Ruth O'Rourke
DTP and Design Coordinator Heather Blagden
Production Editor David Almond
Senior Production Controller Luca Bazzoli
Jacket Coordinator Lucy Philpott
Art Director Maxine Pedliham
Publishing Director Katie Cowan

Illustrator Alicia Rihko

This American Edition, 2022
First American Edition, 2008
Published in the United States by DK Publishing
1745 Broadway, 20th Floor, New York, NY 10019

A catalog record for this book
is available from the Library of Congress.
ISBN 978-0-7440-4013-5

Printed and bound in China

For the curious
www.dk.com

MIX
Paper | Supporting
responsible forestry
FSC™ C018179
www.fsc.org

This book was made with Forest Stewardship Council™ certified paper—one small step in DK's commitment to a sustainable future. For more information go to www.dk.com/our-green-pledge